ALL YOU NEED TO KNOW ABOUT BANKS by Robert Wool
and John A. Cook

THE BUSINESS WRITING HANDBOOK by William C. Paxson

GUERRILLA TACTICS IN THE JOB MARKET by Tom Jackson

HOW TO BUY STOCKS by Louis Engel with Brendan Boyd

MARKETING YOURSELF: THE CATALYST WOMEN'S GUIDE
TO SUCCESSFUL RESUMES AND INTERVIEWS by The Catalyst
Staff

MOLLY'S LIVE FOR SUCCESS by John T. Molloy

NO-NONSENSE MANAGEMENT by Richard S. Sloma

184 BUSINESSES ANYONE CAN START AND MAKE A LOT OF
MONEY by Chase Revel

168 MORE BUSINESSES ANYONE CAN START by Chase Revel

THE ONLY INVESTMENT GUIDE YOU'LL EVER NEED by
Andrew Tobias

SPEAK FOR SUCCESS by Eugene Erlich and Gene R. Hawes

WILLIAM DONOGHUE'S GUIDE TO FINDING MONEY TO
INVEST by William E. Donoghue

YOU CAN NEGOTIATE ANYTHING by Herb Cohen

Marketing Yourself

The catalyst women's guide to successful resumes and interviews

by The Catalyst Staff

Foreword by Sylvia Porter

BANTAM BOOKS

TORONTO • NEW YORK • LONDON • SYDNEY • AUCKLAND

MARKETING YOURSELF

A Bantam Book / published by arrangement with
The Putnam Publishing Group

PRINTING HISTORY

Putnam's edition published June 1980

Bantam edition / September 1981

2nd printing	... February 1982	4th printing	..... January 1984
3rd printing	...... March 1983	5th printing	... November 1984
	6th printing	.... April 1986	

ISBN 0-553-23751-9

Published simultaneously in the United States and Canada

PRINTED IN THE UNITED STATES OF AMERICA

O   15   14   13   12   11   10   9   8   7

ACKNOWLEDGMENTS

Catalyst gives warm thanks to the corporations who provided the funding for this book:

The Sperry and Hutchinson Foundation, Inc.
contributed funding for Part 1: "Resume Preparation"

International Paper Company Foundation
contributed funding for Part 2: "Interviewing to Get the Job You Want"

CONTRIBUTORS

The Catalyst Staff
Carol A. Day, *Vice-President and Director of Publications*
Larayne K. Ewald, *Editor and Researcher*
Maria L. Muniz, *Editor*
Dana L. Topping, *Assistant*

Contributing writers were Tom Jackson for Part 1: "Resume Preparation"; and Linda Small for Part 2: "Interviewing to Get the Job You Want." Advisors for Part 1 for Catalyst were Dee Fensterer and Miriam H. Krohn. Susan Richner served as contributing editor for Part 1.

CONTENTS

Marketing Yourself

FOREWORD

THROUGHOUT THE AGES people have recognized the wisdom of these two words: "Know thyself." And they offer particularly good counsel to job hunters in the 1980s.

You must set your own goals. As a job hunter, you must know your dreams, your skills, your values, your needs. But self-awareness alone is not enough. You must have the skills and information needed to present yourself effectively to potential employers.

Whether you are looking for your first job or making a career change, at some point you will be sending out a resume and someone will interview you. Do you know what to say and how to say it? Do you know what *not* to say—what to leave out of your resume and resist mentioning in the interview? Do you know how to prepare for each job interview? Do you know how to negotiate salary?

Catalyst's new guide for women job hunters, *Marketing Yourself,* will take you through this important process step-by-step.

A Catalyst publication brings with it a decided advantage: The experience and knowledge behind each one are the results of many projects and programs conducted by a solid national organization. For eighteen years Catalyst has been working to help women achieve their career goals. The experience of women Catalyst has assisted has made these women knowledge-able about and sensitive to other women's needs at various stages of career planning and development. Catalyst's publications and services are designed to expand and develop career options for women. And the organization works constantly with employers, educators, counselors, and journalists to heighten awareness of the changing status of women in the work force.

Your career is an important part of your life. As a working woman in the new decade today, you can pursue your own definitions of success and satisfaction. By knowing yourself, and knowing how to present yourself, you will be able to take advantage of new work options with confidence in what you have to offer. The opportunities are now there! Get ready!

Marketing Yourself is your head start.

SYLVIA PORTER

CATALYST: WHAT IT IS, WHY WE WROTE THIS BOOK

Catalyst: Something that brings about a change, that initiates a reaction and enables it to take place. Catalyst, the national nonprofit organization dedicated exclusively to women and their careers, has been creating a climate for change since it was founded in 1962 by its president, Felice N. Schwartz, and five college presidents. With the goal of expanding career opportunities for women, Catalyst has a comprehensive national program that:

- Informs women, employers, counselors, educators, legislators, and the media about issues of common interest through its specialized information center, open to the public.
- Offers career information and guidance to women at all stages of their careers through its more than 150 publications.
- Provides counseling to nearly one million women through its network of more than 200 resource centers nationwide.
- Helps corporate women progress in their careers, and helps employers respond to their needs through its program for employers.
- Offers corporations outstanding women candidates for corporate directorships and assists them with their search through its Corporate Board Resource.

(The Catalyst national headquarters are located at 14 East 60th Street, New York, New York 10022.)

Catalyst's current priorities include addressing the needs in particular of the two-career family, the undergraduate woman, and the upwardly mobile woman. Our role is to facilitate the growing partnership of employers and women by helping women plan their careers and by helping business and industry develop the talent and leadership they need.

INTRODUCTION

WHAT DO job seekers ask about most often?

What do they worry about?

What are the trickiest parts of the job-hunting process?

Resumes and interviews!

Thousands of women at all stages of their careers, from first-time job seekers to top executives, have told us about their problems with preparing a resume or surviving a job interview. This two-part guide is designed to help you master these two essential elements of the job search.

Just as marketing, which the American Marketing Association has defined as "the performance of business activities that direct the flow of goods and services from producer to consumer or user," has become one of the most important and sophisticated elements of contemporary business, marketing can have a special value for women job seekers. They must find the right channels, packaging, outlets, and strategies to market themselves—their skills and experience—to employers. The best way a woman can accomplish this task is to learn how to use the primary tools for marketing herself in the job hunt—successful resumes and interviews.

This book is really two complete volumes in one, part of a continuing series prepared especially for women by Catalyst, the national nonprofit organization that helps women choose, launch, and advance their careers. Part 1, "Resume Preparation," was formerly Catalyst's *Resume Preparation Manual*, a guide that has already helped many thousands of women to create effective resumes that *open doors to interviews*. We are including the manual here so you can use it as a companion to the brand-new interview guide, Part 2 of this book. The interview guide picks up where the resume preparation part ends and explains how to present yourself at the interview so that you can *land the job you want*.

part one

RESUME PREPARATION— A STEP-BY-STEP GUIDE

INTRODUCTION

THIS RESUME PREPARATION PORTION, prepared especially for women, is a unique step-by-step guidebook. It will help you create an effective resume that can open doors to the interviews you want.

To find out just how important a good resume is, we talked to employers across the country. The remarks of Phyllis Hammond, Personnel Director of a medium-sized midwestern publishing firm, are typical of the comments we heard:

> Whenever I advertise to fill a good job, I'm inundated with resumes. I'd like to read them all, but frankly, I don't have the time. Sometimes my assistant spends hours just sorting them into piles—those I should definitely read, borderline cases, and resumes which will get immediate form rejections. You'd be amazed at how many qualified people never make it past my assistant's desk because their resumes are sloppy or unclear.
>
> I think it's particularly important for a woman to have a well-written resume. When a woman is competing for a job, she's often placed under a special magnifying glass. Her qualifications are closely scrutinized and assessed—particularly where a management-level job is at stake. She's got to come across as being very professional or she'll have trouble overcoming some of the negative expectations.
>
> Unfortunately, far too many women just don't know how to write a good resume. They haven't learned how to play up their achievements the way men do. Or they omit valuable work experience because it was work that they didn't get paid for. Very

few women know how to turn their skills and personal experiences into something that an employer can interpret well.

Some other complaints about resumes that we heard from employers were:

- "So many of the ones I see are sloppy and hastily prepared—not the kind of person you'd want to hire."
- "The content is vague and confusing. Applicants have no idea what kinds of jobs they're looking for."
- "Skills and accomplishments are not stressed."
- "There is so much irrelevant information that it is hard to find the important points."
- "The writing style is unclear and hard to follow."
- "Many are just visually unappealing; you can't read them."

Because women face some special problems in the employment world, this guide to resume preparation has been designed by Catalyst to help you. If you go through every step here, you will overcome common resume faults and learn everything you need to know about preparing an effective resume. The ideas, techniques, and approaches we use have been tested by hundreds of job seekers around the country. If you follow each step carefully and thoroughly, you'll end up with a resume that will really work for you.

Before You Begin

When it comes to writing a resume, many people simply grab the nearest pencil, pen, or typewriter, pick up some paper, start at the upper left corner with name and address, and then describe in a rather hasty and unplanned fashion as much as they can about themselves. Others stare for hours at a blank sheet of paper and finally despair of finding anything "meaningful" to say at all.

Even if you've written resumes before, follow our step-by-step approach. Start by defining your job targets, and then progress through a variety of stages until you have a resume that will attract an employer's interest. Because we want you to get the maximum value out of this book, we strongly urge you to stick with it and not skip any of the steps along the way. There's a lot of valuable information here—information that will make the difference between a rejected resume and one that gets you what you want. In short, what we've done is to put together in one guidebook everything you will need to create the resume that presents you in the strongest light.

The Resume—What It Is . . . and Isn't

Let's start with what a resume isn't. It's not your autobiography or your memoirs. It's not a five-page description of everything you've ever done or been involved in. And it's not just a short bare-bones outline of your work experience or a set of sparse descriptions of the jobs you've held.

So what is a resume? It's something you probably never thought it was—an advertisement. That's right. It's an advertisement for you—a well-written, crisply prepared document that persuasively shows what *you* have to "sell" to an employer.

And, like all ads, it has a specific objective to accomplish. Very simply: *The primary purpose of a resume is to get you—its author—interviews with the employers you want to see.*

Since we're talking about advertising, let's look at the competition. In case you didn't already know, it's fierce! There are thousands of job applicants out there, and they all have resumes. Many people are after the same jobs you are. The inevitable result is that only the really good resumes get the attention of potential employers.

We'd like you to get a sense of the challenge involved in making your resume stand out from the pack. Begin by looking at what you have to work with—a blank piece of paper.

Now, suppose someone said that in 250 words or less you had to capture the essence of your work qualifications on that blank paper. Think about it for a moment. Do you know how to make that sheet of paper come alive so that it conveys a positive message about your skills, experience, and accomplishments? Do you know how to turn that blank paper into an invitation for an interview with the employer of your choice?

> *A resume is an advertisement for you; its primary purpose is to get you in to see potential employers about jobs that interest you.*

Can You Transform a Blank Piece of Paper into an Irresistible Advertisement for Yourself? The next eight chapters of this book provide some easy-to-follow steps that will help you.

1 DETERMINING YOUR JOB TARGETS

PREPARING A RESUME without having some idea of your specific job targets is a little like packing for a trip without any idea of where you're going. You'll probably take some things along that you have no need for and leave some important items back home. If you don't have job targets in mind when you write your resume, you'll probably include a lot of irrelevant information and leave out many pertinent facts.

It's much easier to write an effective resume if you know beforehand the kinds of jobs you're looking for.

As you begin to consider job possibilities, be sure you're aware of the large variety of opportunities open to you. The world of work is an immense one, and it's changing all the time. New industries spring up, and old ones slow down. As the economy, technology, and social objectives expand, specific job opportunities grow and change as well. Even in a poor job market, during periods of high unemployment, thousands of new jobs are filled each day.

The big problem with most job seekers is that they look at their job prospects much too narrowly. Often, people look for jobs only in areas in which they are already working, without even considering what else they could or would like to do. This is particularly true with women who have felt locked into positions stereotyped as "feminine" or "women's work." They may be afraid that it isn't right for them to consider some of the more "masculine" job areas such as manufacturers' sales, banking, or industrial management.

As you read this first chapter, you should consider and write down every single job possibility that might interest you. Open your mind to areas you haven't considered before. If there's something you'd like to do but haven't tried, don't automatically discard the idea. You're capable of doing a lot more than you think. Be inventive, expand your perspective, see if you can come up with a dozen or so job situations that normally you might not have considered. Don't worry too much at this point about whether or not you realistically qualify for these positions. You will narrow down your list later. For the moment the idea is to expand your thinking.

Even if you already have a good idea of what your job targets are, this chapter can help you to reinforce your decision. Or it can point you to another area that you might find even more rewarding. The main thing for now is to keep an open mind.

List Your Job Possibilities

Begin by making a list of your job possibilities. Use a special notebook and start out on a page that will be the beginning of your Job Possibilities File. Write down every job title, position, or opportunity you can think of that could possibly be of interest to you. Don't be afraid to put things down that might not directly relate to your own image of yourself. Let your imagination run free. Pretend you're a kid again: What do you want to be when you grow up?

Give yourself a few days to complete this exercise: See if you can come up with twenty-five or thirty different job possibilities in any fields or areas that hold appeal for you. Include the titles of previous jobs only if you want to continue working in those jobs. Fantasize a bit; free associate. You'll find that one idea leads to another. To add to the titles that immediately come to mind, here are some ways that you can come up with even more:

- Carry a notebook around with you and write down every area of work, position, or opportunity that occurs to you or that seems of possible interest.

- Make a point of scanning trade journals or textbooks in any general field that appeals to you. List all work areas that interest you and try to pinpoint some specific job titles.
- Find out if there are any trade or professional associations in fields that interest you. (You can ask people you know or check the directories in the reference room of your local library.) Contact these associations and see what leads they can supply that are related to occupations in the field. (Also, see Part 2 of this book, Chapter 2.)
- Telephone or meet with people working in your areas of interest. Even if you don't know these people very well, you'll probably find that they will enjoy helping you. Ask them for information about the positions in their industries or organizations and add their suggestions to your list.
- Check the Help Wanted sections of newspapers and trade journals, and clip any ads that interest you.

Focusing on Your Job Targets

After you've collected as many possibilities as you can, go back over your list and circle the five jobs that seem to be of most interest to you. Make your choices based on the best combination of interest and practicality. You may change your mind as you develop more ideas later, but don't worry about that now.

From these five jobs select the two that are most relevant to your current campaign, the two for which you would like to prepare a resume. These jobs are now your job targets. Using a separate sheet of paper for each one, list the skills and qualifications that you think an employer would look for in hiring someone to fill the job. Don't concern yourself yet with whether or not *you* have all these qualifications. The idea is to focus on the employer's needs. For example:

Job Target: sales trainee for textile company

Specific skills and abilities sought

by employer:

sales experience	good phone
self confidence	manner
writing skill (reports, letters)	independence
ability to persuade and	sewing,
motivate others	art or design
knowledge of product	courses
and industry	reliability
organizational ability	resourcefulness
teamwork experience	
course in textiles or	
chemistry	
knowledge of community	
public speaking skill	

Keep a folder called Job Possibilities. Include all clippings, news articles, brochures, advertisements, and other information that relate to your job possibilities. It's important to keep expanding this file, adding to your range of job alternatives. Later you'll want to refer back to it when you are ready to narrow down your job targets.

Writing a Help Wanted Advertisement

It's a good idea to put yourself in the role of the employer from time to time because it'll often give you unexpected but important insights about how you can present yourself as a valuable job candidate and how you can better prepare yourself for the job you're seeking.

The next exercise is designed to take you one step further.

Put yourself in the shoes of a potential employer and write a Help Wanted advertisement for one of the two job targets you've chosen. Write the ad as if *you* were trying to recruit a qualified employee. Remember that ads cost money, so use as few words as possible to describe accurately what you, as *employer*, are seeking. Here's an example:

Job Title: Textile sales trainee
self-confident, persuasive individual
with some sales experience. Degree
in textiles or chemistry helpful.
Excellent organizational and writing
skills required. Should be familiar
with local market. Will join an
established sales team, make group
sales presentations, and prepare
reports to management.

In this chapter, you've had the chance to explore a variety of possibilities and to focus on the type of job you're looking for so that your resume writing will be more specifically directed toward your job targets.

As you go through the next chapters in this book and proceed with your job campaign, you may find you want to change your job targets. And that's fine. Your goal is to find the work that suits you; so shift gears as often as you need to. Continue to put new information into your Job Possibilities File in the notebook you've started. Add your own notes, classified advertisements, job leads, and any other information related to your job targets. And remember, keep an open mind about all the kinds of jobs that could interest you.

2 DEVELOPING YOUR PERSONAL BIOGRAPHY

NOW THAT YOU'VE TAKEN a look at where you're heading, you're ready for the second step in preparing your resume: developing your Personal Biography. This is one area in which you are unique. Anyone could have chosen the same job targets you have, but no one else can duplicate your particular experience.

As you go through this chapter, it's important for you to realize that all the skills and expertise you've developed through school, home, and community activities have relevance and value in the work world. That's why we've included some important tools in this chapter to help you examine your background. By the time you finish, you will know what abilities and experience you have to offer to potential employers that will convince them that you should be interviewed.

You can use your notebook again or a file folder for your Personal Biography, which will be a useful permanent record of your experience. You may want to include your school transcripts, old resumes, letters of recommendation, and other pertinent materials in a special Experience File. You should also begin to collect work samples, names and addresses of former employers, references, prior job descriptions, and other items that reflect your life, experience, and skills.

As you work through this chapter and develop your Personal Biography, write down as much information as possible about yourself. This record is *your* personal inventory, so be sure to include everything, no matter how obvious a given aspect of your history may seem. Complete each item without being constrained by what you think you ought to write. Consider everything you have done at home, in the community, at school, and in other experiences, including paying jobs or unpaid (volunteer) work. The phrasing of your entries is not terribly important at this point. You're still in the exploratory stages and will get to the actual resume wording in a later chapter.

In compiling your Personal Biography, you may find it useful to talk to your friends, family, and former business associates. They can often help you to remember important information that you might otherwise overlook.

PERSONAL BIOGRAPHY

1. Education

Begin with your education. On a fresh sheet of paper in your notebook, list the following:

High School
- Name and address of your high school
- Year you graduated

College
- Name and address of your college
- Year you graduated (or the number of credits you completed, if you didn't graduate)
- Type of degree earned
- College major
- College minor

Graduate or Professional School
- Name and address of graduate or professional school
- Year you graduated (or number of credits completed)

- Type of degree earned
- Major
- Minor

Other
- Describe

This information is an outline of your educational experience. Now, consider those years in more depth. The following questions were designed to help you analyze this part of your life. As you write your answers, take your time and go into as much detail as you like.

- During your education, which subjects did you like best? Why?
- Which subjects did you like least? Why?
- Were your grades best in your major? If no, explain.
- Have you taken (or are you now taking) any extension, adult education, or other courses? If so, what are they, and why did you become interested in them?
- Would you now be interested in further training or specialized courses to help you in your career? Any comments?
- Describe your extracurricular activities while in school, and underline the ones that still interest you.
- What three achievements in school made you most proud?
- Did you hold any jobs during your school years? During summers between school years? If so, list each position and your duties.

Now you have completed step one of your Personal Biography. Is there anything else related to your education that might be worth noting? If so, write it down.

2. Hobbies/Pastimes/Interests

Your Personal Biography should also include all those things that you do simply for fun. In step two you will examine your leisure activities—your hobbies, pastimes, and interests.

Begin with a fresh sheet of paper (or a new page in your notebook). List everything, past and present, even activities that may seem unimportant to your career. And go beyond the general category. For example, instead of just saying "movies," be more specific, adding "read about movie history," "make home movies," etc. If sailing is your interest, be specific: "competed in amateur races," "maintained sailboat," etc.

In this category it is particularly important to be open in your thinking. Include all personal interests that are important to you. Don't omit a particular interest because you feel it would be of no value to an employer. Remember, this Personal Biography is being prepared without specific regard to what will later be used in your resume.

After each interest, note the number of years you have been involved with it and how good you are at it—your level of competence. For example, are you a beginner at skiing, or extremely proficient? Do you sew a little, or design your own wardrobe?

Once you've listed all your interests, take a few minutes to think about this question. Do you see any work applications for any of your hobbies or interests (with or without further training)? Many times hobbies are clues to what you are really good at and interested in—and to the kind of job you should consider. One woman whose hobby was photography found a job working on educational filmstrips. If you see any possible job applications in your list of interests, write them down as part of your Personal Biography.

Now let's try an experiment. Go back and look again at what you have written under hobbies and pastimes. Imagine that one or two of these hobbies belong to someone else. Invent a possible work application for each one, and list them with the others. (This step might help you to be more objective about your experiences.)

3. Membership in Organizations—Past and Present

The groups that you've joined also are clues to your job potential. For step three, list all the organizations to which you belong or have belonged. Include civic, political, cultural, feminist, professional, and social groups of every kind: esoteric, intellectual, exercise, community, etc. And briefly note the degree of your involvement in each activity. Why is it important to you? What have you learned from it?

4. Skills

The skills you have acquired over the years are an essential part of your Personal Biography. In step four, list any specific skills you have developed as a result of formal or informal training or experience. For example, driving, writing, speaking, furniture refinishing, photography, as well as financial planning, programming, or any other skill you have developed in your working or nonworking life. We've listed some skills for your convenience, but be sure to add to our list any others that you think of.

For each skill, try to rate your degree of competence—are you excellent, very good, good, or still a novice? Then note where and when and how this skill was demonstrated. Don't confine yourself to on-the-job situations. You may repeat any of your hobbies or educational experiences here. Who says you can't enjoy work? You can set up your notebook page to look like this.

Skill	Degree of Competence			Comments
(list)	Excellent	Very Good	Good	

Talking
Writing
Selling
Teaching
Supervising
Editing
Motivating
Listening
Languages (specify)
Painting
Performing
Composing
Creative Writing
Designing
Dancing
Acting
Sewing
Decorating
Inventing
Landscaping
Cooking
Studying
Researching
Conceptualizing with numbers
Conceptualizing with ideas
Analyzing
Synthesizing
Problem solving
Decision making
Managing
Negotiating
Typing
Carpentry
Mechanical
Drafting
Driving
Gardening
Repairing

As you went through this exercise you probably thought of other skills that you have. Take some time and list them too.

5. Jobs

The final step in compiling your Personal Biography is to describe your work experience. It's essential that you include *all* your jobs—both paid and unpaid, long-term or temporary.

You might find it helpful to put the following headings at the top of your page:

Chronology				*Contributions*
Year	Organization	Title Activity	Salary	Most significant contributions to employer

---

Now, make a full entry for each job or unpaid work experience. Begin with the most recent year you worked and list backward, year by year, to a maximum of ten years. If your job experience in recent years has been brief or nonexistent, include some of your earlier paid or unpaid work.

Write down the organization, title, and salary for each year worked, even though some of the years might be identical or very similar. And be sure to include all jobs (full- or part-time) even if they do not represent your current field of interest. If you were a housewife for some or all of these years and did not have outside work, see if you can translate this experience into work-related terms. If you are a recent or near graduate, be sure to indicate all your summer jobs and any part-time work you had during your school years, even though you have already listed them in this Personal Biography.

Then describe the most significant contributions you made in your work for each year. What did you accomplish? What did you learn? What did the organization as a whole accomplish? (Remember, *your* participation contributed to this accomplishment.) Include things that you may have done as part of a team. You may want to spend some extra time on this step and perhaps to refer to old job descriptions, recommendations, or samples of your work.

Now reread what you've written and, in 50 words or less, summarize what you feel are your most important contributions. Pretend that you are writing a Situation Wanted newspaper advertisement for yourself, an ad that a potential employer would read. Here's a sample:

> Specialist in landscape design and garden development seeks full-time position. Have five years' experience in designing for broad acreage, rockeries, roof gardens, in domestic and commercial settings. Established and maintained local clinic, prepared instructional materials, and created innovative maintenance programs.

In your notebook, write your own Situation Wanted ad. You might want to refer back to earlier steps in your Personal Biography for additional insights. Now go back and read your advertisement again. Does it present you in a positive way? Women are often reluctant to project themselves in a strong, assertive manner that emphasizes their special abilities. They're sometimes afraid of being considered too aggressive. That kind of feeling could get in *your* way, so remember that in the job market it is no longer appropriate and doesn't make sense to be overly modest about your skills. Take another look now at your background and see if you can sell yourself still more effectively. Try another Situation Wanted ad.

It may have been a long time since you've looked at your skills and experiences so objectively. We hope you have now discovered or been reminded of some important strengths. You are now in a better position to market yourself, because you have identified your capabilities and can see the full range of what you have to offer employers.

As you go through the next chapters, continue to look at your experiences in terms of their value to a potential employer. Don't be afraid to examine the relevance of your background for positions in areas that are usually dominated by men. As a woman you may have had jobs with plenty of responsibility but not much rank or recognition. Take a close look at these experiences so you can identify aspects of the work or involvement that could be translated beneficially into your current job targets.

And remember to *document* your abilities. Collect and file your college transcripts, work samples, letters of recommendation, names and addresses of references, or anything else related to your prior experience that is relevant to your job campaign. Keep them with or in your notebook.

If you haven't done so already, write away for those records you may need, call the people who would be willing to write references for you, and make copies of important work samples. Keep adding information to your Personal Biography and file as you progress through this manual and conduct your job search.

3 ANALYZING YOUR ACHIEVEMENTS

IN THE LAST CHAPTER you developed your Personal Biography and made some insights about your skills. What employers need to know is whether *your* skills can be used to solve *their* problems. That's what an employer is really looking for— someone who can solve the specific problems that occur on the job.

Take an example of a skill—writing—and consider how it becomes increasingly valuable when it has been used in a work environment to solve problems. Say an employer wants to hire a writer in the marketing department, and you have writing skills. You're obviously a good candidate. But what the employer really wants to know is whether you can use your writing skill to successfully prepare the company's marketing brochures in a way that gets results.

Could you deal with salespeople to get specific information? Would you be able to work with the production staff to see that the brochure is printed on time? Can you adapt your writing style to the kind of copy that really sells? In other words, writing is not just an isolated skill; it has to be used in conjunction with other skills to solve a specific problem.

If you've already written a marketing brochure for another company, or written an article about marketing, or produced a brochure about another organization's operations, you're a much more valuable candidate because you've proven to employers that you can use your writing skill to solve particular problems.

In this chapter you're going to look at what you've actually done with your skills so that you'll be able to present them on your resume in terms of problem-solving capabilities. Anytime you've used a skill to solve a problem, you've achieved something, and in this chapter you'll be looking at all your achievements to see how they can relate to a prospective employer's needs.

If you haven't worked before, or if your career has been interrupted, you may be tempted to take a backseat role—"No, I haven't accomplished much that would be useful in the career marketplace. I spent most of my time at home" is a familiar lament. Well, enough of that. On these pages, you're going to take a look at the importance of all your achievements. Achievements and accomplishments, no matter where they took place, provide important clues about your potential for success—a potential that should be instantly visible on that ordinary printed page called your resume.

Achievements Analysis

Let's examine the word "achievement." The Random House *Dictionary of the English Language* defines an achievement as *"the final accomplishment of something noteworthy after much effort and often in spite of obstacles."* An achievement differs from a skill or capability in that it is a finished act and an end result, whereas a skill or capability might exist but might never have been put to a significant use.

Notice the last words in the box below: "work and nonwork life." Nonwork activities are very important. If you use your imagination, you'll see that many functions you perform in your personal life will have real value in the "outside" world. Your skills and abilities are the common denominator between nonwork activities and jobs.

> Some of your
> *education/skills/interests/hobbies/jobs*
> come together as
> *problem-solving capabilities,*
> and for some of them you will recall actual occasions of
> *accomplishment and achievement*
> in your work and nonwork life.

Look at the following examples of some nonwork accomplishments, and see how they translate into work equivalents.

Nonwork Accomplishment	Demonstrated Skills	Work Equivalent
Managed campaign for community center	aggressiveness political savvy writing ability supervisory ability	Fund raiser/customer relations/sales management/public relations
Organized nonprofit food cooperative	mathematical ability organizational ability persistence follow-through	Purchasing agent/store manager/office systems
Became accomplished dancer	dancing persistence energy coordination	Physical therapist (paraprofessional)/exercise instructor/modeling/or dance instructor

Now take a look at some of your own accomplishments, with a view toward analyzing them and distilling the problem-solving skills and capabilities that made them possible. Experience shows that by going through this exercise, you will be able to gain important insights into the qualities you have that could make an employer notice you—and call you for an interview!

Many people make the mistake of describing what they did in a work situation in terms of their duties or their job descriptions. This way of describing work is not nearly so powerful as describing your experience in terms of what you accomplished. For example, let's say that your duties were to coordinate development of new sales brochures, work with writing and production staff, and help to prepare marketing strategy.

Here's how these same duties might be stated in terms of your actual accomplishments:

> Developed ten new sales brochures in two years, four of which helped bring in sales in excess of $500,000 (more than double the companywide average).

Try another example. Your duty was to recruit new voluteers for a community hospital. This function could be presented more impressively in the following manner:

> Devised intensive program of contacting youth groups to recruit volunteers at local hospital. Increased number of volunteers by more than 25 percent in one year.

Here are some examples of other accomplishments that women using this book have listed:

- Conceived and organized freshman orientation program.
- Ran personnel department during director's extended absence.
- Wrote a training manual that increased operator efficiency 20 percent.
- Designed a rock garden.
- Remodeled an old barn.

- Supported three children by doing free-lance writing and copy-editing.
- Obtained a master's degree in nutrition while also earning a living at a full-time job.
- Reorganized campus theater group into repertory company.

1. List Your Achievements

Now it's your turn. On a sheet of paper, list a minimum of five specific events (personal, school, community, or work) that you feel represented accomplishments, and don't worry if they aren't earthshaking. This is step one of your Achievements Analysis. It makes it easier if you use an action verb like the ones listed below to begin each sentence.

designed	sold
researched	expanded
trained	developed
supervised	planned
contracted	managed
improved	created
implemented	presented
established	organized
analyzed	negotiated
invented	administered
directed	conducted
reduced costs	prepared
wrote	

2. Analyze Your Achievements

The next step is to analyze the achievements you've just listed. Consider them one by one and then list the skills or personal attributes that you think enabled you to accomplish each task. In each case ask yourself: What is there about me that made it possible to accomplish this? Think about your personality as well as your specific skills and abilities. Traits that affect your accomplishments might include willingness to work hard, patience, ability to handle people, sales ability, organizing ability, knowledge of antiques, ability to sketch, logical thinking, dynamic presentation, or virtually any other skill or capability. List anything you can think of that contributed to your success in each achievement.

Here's an example of step two:

Achievement: increased number of volunteers at local hospital by more than 25 percent.
Problem solving capabilities and skills: organizational skills, good public speaker, sales ability, hard work, capacity to motivate people, ability to overcome resistance.

Now analyze five of the achievements you listed in your notebook in step one of your Achievements Analysis.

3. Identify Your Skills

Now sit back and review the results. What attributes, skills, or abilities show up most frequently? For step three, select the four or five skills that are repeated the most, and list them in your notebook in order of frequency.

4. List Additional Skills

Now think whether there are any other important problem-solving skills that didn't show up. If so, list them.

You are almost halfway through this part of the guidebook now, and have completed the self-examination section. Because of your investment in this process, you should have a pretty clear idea of your strongest selling points; you're in a good position to start working directly on your resume.

From this point everything presented will directly relate to the actual writing of the resume. As we mentioned earlier, your resume is your most important sales piece. And as in most effective sales and marketing presentations, preparation is often ten times more involved and lengthy than the end result.

4 *CHOOSING YOUR RESUME FORMAT*

EVEN THOUGH THERE are a number of very important and specific rules for writing a resume, there is no one "right" resume style or format. The right format for you is the one that works and gets you an interview. What works for you may be totally unsuitable for someone else.

Choosing the most appropriate format is sometimes difficult for women whose experience is limited or whose job experience does not fit into neat little time periods. For example, suppose you took several years off to raise a family after having held down a responsible job before you were married. How do you emphasize your work experience and not the gap in your work background? This chapter examines the advantages and disadvantages of three common resume formats and one alternative style so that you can consider which format will work best for you.

Before you examine the resume samples on the following pages, take a moment to reemphasize in your mind the major objective of your resume: *to get you interviews.* The resume achieves this objective by clearly presenting key information about you and by accentuating skills, abilities, and accomplishments that will attract the attention of a potential employer. Keep these objectives in mind as you choose your format.

The three most common resume formats are:

The Chronological Resume
The Functional Resume
The Combination Resume

(If none of these suits your needs, there's one more possibility—the Resume Alternative, described on page 58.)

The Chronological Resume

The chronological resume is the most widely accepted resume format and the one with which employers are most familiar. It also is the easiest to write. Jobs are listed in reverse chronological order, starting with the most *recent* (which generally receives the greatest emphasis), and working back through the years.

Employment dates are usually listed first, followed by name of organization and then job title. You may be expected to give both month and year of employment, but short gaps probably won't be questioned until the interview.

The chronological resume has several advantages:

- Professional interviewers are more familiar with it.
- It is the easiest to prepare, since its content is structured by familiar dates, companies, and titles.
- A steady employment record (without much job hopping) is put into the best perspective.
- It provides the interviewer with a guide for discussing work experience.

The chronological resume has some disadvantages:

- It can starkly reveal employment gaps.
- It may put undesired emphasis on job areas that an applicant wants to minimize.
- Skill areas are difficult to spotlight unless they are reflected in the most recent job.

Chronological Resume

This is a typical chronological resume. It shows major responsibilities as well as a diversity of experience. There are no employment gaps.

Roberta Simon
415 High Street
Portland, Oregon 97201
(503) 555–4183

Staff Assistant

Work Experience:

1971–Present

Staff Assistant to Chairman,
Department of Sociology
University of Oregon
Responsible for smooth day-to-day running of
department of 15 persons.

- Prepare university and government surveys and reports.
- Prepare agenda and faculty meeting minutes.
- Authorize expenditures of $175,000 budget.
- Analyze quantity audits, projections, and financial statements.
- Interpret and apply university and government policies.

1969–1971

Assistant to Chairman,
Math Department
Portland State University

- Carried out administrative policies of section—processed payroll, coordinated work schedules, ordered supplies and equipment.
- Scheduled meetings and appointments.

1968–1969

Secretary/Editor, *Journal of Applied Math*

- Directed day-to-day journal operation.
- Handled all general queries with authors.
- Served as liaison between authors and publisher.
- Prepared statistics, agenda, and minutes of editors' meetings.

Education:

B.A. Portland State University, 1968. Humanities major. Honor Student.

The Functional Resume

The functional resume is organized to highlight the qualifications of the applicant, with little emphasis on specific dates.

The functional resume has some distinct advantages:

- It stresses selected skill areas that are marketable or in demand.
- It helps camouflage a spotty employment record.
- It allows the applicant to emphasize professional growth.
- Positions not related to current career goals can be played down.

The functional resume also has some disadvantages:

- Many employers are suspicious of it, and will want to see additional work-history information.
- It doesn't allow you to highlight companies or organizations for which you've worked.

Functional Resume

This applicant worked for a number of years on a free-lance basis as a consultant for various government departments and private agencies. She has chosen a functional resume to play down the large number of different assignments, which she feels she could best handle at the interview.

Ms. Alice Hunt
125 West 89th Street
New York, New York 10024
(212) 555-0600 (office)
(212) 555-3878

Major Work Experience

(1965-1976)

Program Development

Conducted research into the representation of minority students in medical colleges. Developed proposal for a major study in the field. Secured funding for the project; coordinated and administered the program and assumed responsibility for accountability of $845,000. Program has had major effect on medical education.

Initiated and developed a national minority student recruitment program for 20 medical colleges.

Writing

Compiled and published reports in a variety of educational areas. Produced several booklets on urban problems for general distribution.

Research

Gathered and analyzed information concerning higher education in a variety of specialized fields. Familiar with data collection and statistics. Good knowledge of computers.

Administration and Management

Hired and trained research assistants. Managed medium-sized (30 people) office.

Public Relations

Prepared press releases and conducted press conferences.

Education

Barnard College, B.A. English Literature, 1958
Columbia University, M.A. Journalism, 1959

The Combination Format

The combination resume is similar in format to the functional resume; however, company names and dates are included in a separate section.

The combination format allows an applicant to stress the preferred and most relevant skill areas, and at the same time satisfies the employer's desire to know names and dates. The combination format has the following advantages:

- It provides a good opportunity to emphasize the applicant's most relevant skills and abilities.
- Gaps in employment can be de-emphasized.
- It can be varied to emphasize chronology and de-emphasize functional descriptions, or vice versa.

There is one distinct disadvantage:

- The Combination Format takes longer to read, and an employer can lose interest unless it is very succinctly written and attractively laid out.

Combination Format

Because her experience is chiefly with one firm, this applicant's best resume type is a combined chronological-functional resume. It highlights the areas of her experience that she considers most important, and only touches on earlier experience, which at this time in her career is not so significant.

Jane Hardwick
1736 D Street N.W.
Washington, D.C. 20006
(202) 555-8192

Sales Management: Responsible for planning and directing sales program for several divisions. Made major policy decisions in all phases of sales activities. Successfully built sales 85 percent above preceding year's business.

Market Planning: Investigated the market for new products and analyzed new markets for established product lines. Introduced new chewing gum package for supermarkets, following a marketing study recommendation.

Merchandising: Through close liaison with merchandising executives in major chains, developed point-of-purchase displays which gave added shelf space to company products. Coordinated merchandising and advertising programs with stores.

Sales Training: Hired and trained numerous merchandisers and salespersons. Established formal company sales training program.

Sales: Maintained close personal contact with buyers in major supermarket outlets. Have personally sold products to chains all over the U.S.

1964–Present Acme Chewing Gum Company—

Started as Sales Representative and worked through sales ranks to current position of District Manager in 1971.

1960–1964 Sucrose Company—

Sold candy to supermarkets, drug, and variety chains and vending machine companies. Covered Florida, Georgia, and Alabama. Opened 32 new accounts in first year. Generated $72,000 in new orders—the highest ever attained by a new sales representative.

Education: B.A., Florida State College 1960

What to Leave Out

We'd like to add a word about a few items that do not belong in your resume, no matter which format you choose. Anything that does not contribute to getting you an interview should be eliminated. For example, the names and ages of your children, leisure-time activities that have nothing to do with your job targets, and lists of personal friends as references. All these tend to clutter the resume and detract from essential information you want to get across.

As for the often-used statement at the top of the resume about "Position Desired" or "Job Objective," remember that it could greatly limit your range of job possibilities. Usually the best place to emphasize your interest in a particular job is in the cover letter that accompanies your resume. (See Chapter 8.)

The Resume Alternative

Outside of certain entry-level and clerical positions, and most blue-collar jobs, the resume is the basic door opener. There are, however, a few exceptions, particularly if:

- You have been out of the labor force for an extended period of time, without activities directly related to the world of paid employment. Your time may have been spent as a housewife with few outside involvements, as a person with extended leisure travel, as an unpublished writer, or as a convalescent from prolonged illness or incapacitation.
- You have been involved throughout most of your career in work that holds no further interest for you. You may want to get away from being typecast as a bookkeeper, teacher, or secretary, for example, and move into management training or another field of work.

In such cases, and in others where you feel that a resume could stand in the way of getting an interview with an employer you wish to see, you might consider what we call the Resume Alternative—a well-prepared, highly informative letter to a specific person at a company or organization that interests you. The objective of this letter is to emphasize your specific skills and accomplishments and to show how they apply to the employer's needs. The Resume Alternative also provides an opportunity to make a direct and personal pitch based on your detailed research and analysis into an organization's needs.

If you have good references who would be known to the employer, be a name dropper. Mention their names as close to the opening of the letter as possible. Also include any of your present or former business or organizational affiliations that are relevant. The writer of the following letter does this well:

1722 Napa Drive
Sonoma, California 95476
(213) 555–2596
March 1, 1980

Mr. Alex B. Cowan
Med-Search Inc.
425 La Brea Drive
Pacific Dunes, California 92316

Dear Mr. Cowan:

Dr. Paul Parish at the USC Graduate School suggested that I contact you about the studies your firm is currently making into the utilization of nursing homes in this country. He also remarked that you might be thinking about hiring someone to coordinate the field investigations that are part of your study.

As an officer of our local Women's Community Center, I have had a great deal of experience with the operation of day-care centers, which, as you know, are quite similar in administration to nursing homes. This experience includes familiarity with the financial and administration aspects of the centers as well as knowledge of the programming and educational considerations. I have met with the staffs of most of the day-care centers in the county, and am certain that my ability to work with these professionals would enable me to facilitate the execution of your study.

In addition to this experience, I have had two years of administrative work on an important research project in health care at USC while working on my master's degree in education.

I plan to be near your office next week and wonder if we could get together on Wednesday or Thursday for an interview. I'll call you to confirm when you will be available.

Yours truly,

Diane Sims

Diane Sims

Notice how Diane Sims was able to create interest in her ability by showing her knowledge of the employer's needs and her potential for meeting them. Notice, too, that she suggested specific dates for meeting in the near future, a suggestion that underscores her interest in getting the job. In sales parlance, Ms. Sims is making an important step toward "closing the sale."

A Resume Alternative could be longer than the one shown here if additional information would attract attention and persuade a potential employer. Be concise, however. You should be sure to follow the rules of good resume writing described in this guidebook because, even in a letter format, you must try to identify the needs of the employer and indicate how your abilities and accomplishments can address those needs. Your problem-solving skills will stimulate the employer's interest in you.

Now let's go over the choices again and briefly summarize their advantages. The *chronological resume,* the most familiar format, puts a steady employment record into the best perspective; the *functional resume* emphasizes major areas of strength and experience, and plays down employment dates; the *combination resume* combines major areas of expertise with the dates and places of employment. The *Resume Alternative* is a well-structured letter that should be used in special situations where a resume might not be appropriate, or where a more direct pitch might be the most effective approach.

When you're satisfied with your choice of format, you're ready to proceed with Chapter Five—choosing the words and phrases that will best convey a sense of who you are and what you've accomplished.

5 SELECTING WORDS AND PHRASES THAT ADVERTISE YOUR SKILLS

NOW IT'S TIME to give that blank piece of paper its first breath of life. This isn't as easy as it sounds. If you shape and mold it the right way, your resume will become a vital sales piece for you, a document that presents your accomplishments and says "Read me!" to any prospective employer. If you don't put this next necessary effort into your resume, it will become just another dull, ineffectual resume that gets put to one side of someone's desk.

This chapter looks at the writing *style* you will use—the words and phrases you will select to make your resume lively and informative. Here are some basic guidelines you can follow:

1. Use action words in short, clearly written phrases.
2. Use the minimum number of words necessary to convey accurately what you wish to say.
3. Select words that will mean something to the person who will read your resume. Use the jargon of your chosen field where appropriate.
4. Avoid introductory phrases such as "my duties included" or "I was in charge of the section which. . . ." Start right out with the key benefits you can convey to an employer—such things as:

- Saved $100,000.
- Designed a better system.
- Organized political campaign.
- Created community programs.

5. List accomplishments whenever possible rather than just describing duties.
6. Avoid extraneous information and don't try to convey too many ideas at once. You'll only dilute your key selling points.
7. Always keep the needs of a potential employer in mind; in your resume, put them ahead of your own desires and concerns.

Some Words and Phrases to Use

In Chapter 3 we asked you to write five accomplishments beginning with a series of action words. Now you're going to expand on this list and create some of the phrases you could actually use in your resume. Following is a sample list of effective words to use in your resume. They are powerful, action-oriented words.

designed	was awarded	expanded
improved	prepared	presented
researched	maintained	negotiated
implemented	oversaw	organized
trained	handled	operated
established	taught	evaluated
supervised	directed	exhibited
analyzed	developed	supported
contracted	reduced costs	reorganized
invented	planned	cut
administered	wrote	edited
conducted	managed	produced
was promoted	sold	contacted
	created	

Notice how well these words can be used to introduce good resume phrases:

• Reorganized the entire work flow of the office, increasing output significantly.

- Oversaw maintenance of $3 million worth of equipment.
- Wrote four publications in the field.
- Maintained all department sales records and performance targets.
- Developed new procedures to . . .
- Prepared bibliography on environmental hazards.
- Handled finances, organized meetings, and directed activities of 50 men and women.
- Taught two undergraduate courses while completing Ph.D. work.
- Designed and implemented innovative inventory system.
- Cut production time by 20 percent.
- Created a new product image and sold this concept to the marketing committee.

Now it's your turn. In the following exercise, create phrases pertaining to your own skills and abilities, each phrase beginning with one of the action words shown below. You may have to search your memory a bit to find accomplishments that fit each of the words listed. At first glance you may think that you never designed or analyzed or organized anything, but if you stop for a few moments you will realize that you have. The point is to come up with as many personal "sales points" as you can. See if you can write phrases for at least 10 of the words below, and if possible stretch your imagination to fill in all 15.

designed	established	sold
improved	supervised	planned
researched	analyzed	organized
implemented	wrote	evaluated
trained	conducted	was promoted

Before you move on, take time to review some of the job advertisements that you have collected in your Job Possibilities File to see what words and phrases potential employers are using in their ads. See if you want to incorporate some of these words into the resume, which you're now ready to start writing. Turn to Chapter 6, where you'll begin your first draft.

6 PREPARING YOUR FIRST DRAFT

At last!

Now that you have determined your Job Targets, developed your Personal Biography, analyzed your achievements, chosen a format, and written some action-packed phrases about your experience, you're ready to prepare the first draft of your resume.

Don't attempt to make your resume look good on the first try. It's virtually impossible. Reconcile yourself to the fact that you will have to write two or three drafts before you develop a resume that is complete and easy to read, has an attractive layout, communicates your abilities, and makes the recipient want to interview you.

How to Prepare the First Draft

To begin, in your notebook divide several sheets of paper in half with a horizontal line. You will use these divided pages to draft sections of your resume. Plan to use one for each important position—paying or nonpaying—and one for every skill area and for every major segment of education or experience that is relevant to your job objectives.

Review your Personal Biography and Achievements Analysis. Sort out the major items that you think are most appropriate for use on your resume. Transfer each of these items to the top of one sheet of paper and write down and fill in as many details as are relevant on the top half of the page. Then add to this information any additional facts required to complete the picture of that item. Next, review the words and phrases that you have written. Use the bottom half of the page to edit the information into concise, hard-hitting paragraphs.

Remember, stress your *accomplishments* and the benefits they convey. Finally, write these paragraphs with an actual recipient in mind. On the following page you can see how one applicant described a specific job experience.

Step One: Assemble Information

(The instructions are to assemble as much information as possible, and include it in the space provided.)

Category covered: Reader's Digest 1970–1974

Researched comparative costs of advertising in major magazine competitors of Reader's Digest.

Disseminated my findings to media sales people and the promotional department

Wrote and distributed a biweekly newspaper to marketing people regarding trends in the industry.

Hired and trained another writer to work on this project.

Worked with the promotion department to produce marketing material based on this information.

Reported to marketing director.

Step Two: Condense That Information

(The instructions are to condense the above information into an interesting resume paragraph.)

Analyzed comparative costs of advertising in major competitors of Reader's Digest.
Developed promotional material based on this information.
Established a revised communications network to advise media sales people of major trends in this area.

Here's another example of how to transform notes into resume paragraphs. Look at the following notes taken from the step one section of the resume drafting exercise for Roberta Simon's resume. Compare these notes with her finished resume paragraph for the same job.

Category covered: Dept. of Sociology, Univ. of Oregon—1971–present

Title was Staff Assistant. I was in charge of all logistics and the running of the department (administrative area), including supervision of clerks, two secretaries, and five others —

I made sure that all government reports, surveys, and other requested pieces of information were compiled and released to the appropriate authorities on time, and correctly. Was in charge of keeping minutes of faculty meetings. — Processed all requests from departments for the authorization to expand funds. Was in charge of all budget matters.

Now it's time to make similar notes for each area of information you plan to use in your actual resume. Use as many sheets of paper in your notebook as you need. Follow step one and step two for each category.

Completing Your First Draft

Review your own resume paragraphs. Continue editing and rewriting until you are satisfied that you have written a good advertisement for yourself.

You are now ready to combine the individual final paragraphs of your resume drafting exercise into a full resume. As you prepare this draft, it's time to start thinking about how to lay it out in the most readable fashion.

The minute a professional advertisement is written, it goes to the art department for design and layout. Before it is released to the public, it must be attractive to look at, and the key points must stand out crisply and succinctly. The same is true for your resume. Interviewers are inundated with forms, letters, reports, and other resumes. If your resume is poorly typed or crowded, or if it is too long or its salient points are difficult to pick out, you run the risk of having it overlooked. People skip unappealing ads. So it is your goal to be sure that your resume stands out from the rest and gets read.

Here are some important tips about resume layout:

- Single-space your resume and keep the total length to a page or two. *One page is preferable!* Employers tell us that resumes over one page have a reduced chance of being carefully read.
- Retain an attractive amount of "white space": Leave at least one-inch margins, double-space between paragraphs, and allow at least one inch at the top and bottom of the page.
- Keep paragraphs short, no more than eight or ten lines.
- Break up long ideas into short sentences or phrases.
- Emphasize each new category of information (Education, Work Experience, etc.) in such a way that readers can quickly find the specific information they seek.
- Avoid unnecessary and obvious captions, such as "Name" and "Address."

And follow this general rule: The layout of the resume should contribute to your objective of getting an employer to invite you for an interview.

7 CRITIQUING AND MAKING FINAL REVISIONS

THERE IS SOMETHING absolute about that word "final." Taken from the Latin *finis,* it literally means the end. During Chapter 6 you may have become anxious to finish your resume, to hurry out and have it typed and printed. But most likely rushing the final product, on which you have lavished so much attention, is a mistake.

Before a company introduces a new product in "final" form to the public, it generally invests quite a bit of money to test market that product. Consumers in the test-market area frequently provide invaluable comments about how the product can be improved; their feedback can virtually make or break that new product. So it should be with your resume. The feedback you'll get from friends and from people in the field will provide you with the finishing touches, those important last-minute revisions that may mean the difference between just another resume and one that really succeeds.

In this chapter you'll have the opportunity to sit at the critic's desk. First you'll rate a sample resume, and then you'll critique your own. Finally, you'll test market your resume by showing it to other people who can give you valuable criticism.

By the time you finish this chapter, you will have accomplished four objectives:

1. Made certain that your resume communicates your strengths so that they will relate to the needs of potential employers.

2. Eliminated all extraneous words, phrases, and information from your resume.
3. Settled on an attractive layout using margins, spacing, headings, underlining, capitals, and white space, so as to produce a clear, inviting, and professional resume.
4. Polished the writing so that it conveys the information you want.

The Resume Critique Form

The form on page 75 was designed especially for use with this book. Make several copies (photocopying will save you time) to use for your own and others' critiques of your resume. (Of course, you can simply ask for an oral critique, but the form is convenient and will ensure that all the important points are covered.)

The Process of Critiquing

Before you begin your job as a resume critic, put yourself in the right frame of mind. You are a busy employer. It's 10:30 in the morning and you have already looked at 65 resumes. You have 25 more to screen before an 11 A.M. meeting with your department head. So you really have to be quick and critical with the pile in front of you.

O.K.—in the role? Now get ready; we've provided a copy of the resume of Ms. Becky Conway for you to critique on page 76. (The resume is real. Only the name has been changed to protect the innocent!) Read the resume and make your comments about how it could be improved, using one of your copies of the Resume Critique Form on page 75. When you have finished your turn as critic, take a look at page 77 to see how we critiqued Ms. Conway's resume.

Resume Critique Form

Rate the resume on the points shown below, scoring from a low of 1 to a high of 3 in each of the categories listed. Then score and compare your rating against the highest possible total score of 30. Write comments for each category receiving a score of less than 3.

Item	Score 1	2	3	How It Could Be Improved
1 **Overall appearance.** Do you want to read it?				
2 **Layout.** Does the resume look professional, well typed and printed, with good margins, etc. Do key sales points stand out?				
3 **Length.** Could the resume tell the same story if it were shortened?				
4 **Relevance.** Has extraneous material been eliminated?				
5 **Writing Style.** Is it easy to get a picture of the applicant's qualifications?				
6 **Action Orientation.** Do sentences and paragraphs begin with action verbs?				
7 **Specificity.** Does resume avoid generalities and focus on specific information about experience, projects, products, etc.?				
8 **Accomplishments.** Are applicant's accomplishments and problem-solving skills emphasized?				
9 **Completeness.** Is all important information included?				
10 **Bottom Line.** How well does the resume accomplish its ultimate purpose of getting the employer to invite the applicant in for an interview?				

Rating Point Total _____ (Out of a maximum of 30)

What are some other ways that you would suggest to improve this resume?

_____

_____

Becky Conway
1875 Riverside Drive
Macon, Georgia (404) 555–4003

Date of Birth: 3-19-35
Place of Birth: Atlanta, Georgia
Marital Status: Divorced
Social Security Number: 652 46 5043
U.S. Citizen
Health: Excellent

EDUCATION

1966   Oglethorpe University, Atlanta, Georgia (Kindergarten methods)
1953–1954   Emory University, Atlanta, Georgia (Pre-med)
1949–1953   Sandy Springs High School, Atlanta, Georgia
1941–1949   James L. Riley Elementary School, Atlanta, Georgia

In addition, I have attended library workshops at a number of Georgia universities in General Adult Books, Story Hours, Teenage and Children's Books, and Summer Programs. I have also attended many workshops and training programs in psychology and anthropology.

I speak, read, and write Spanish fluently.

EMPLOYMENT

1967–Present   Professional Assistant, Macon Public Library, Macon, Georgia. Major duties: book selection, reference, book orders, book reviews, checking books out to public, and story-hour supervision.
1966–1967   Teacher, Help Line. In addition to teaching activities, I was involved in overall planning, organization, and counseling of parents of children in all classes in the local program.
1955–1961   Interpreter, U.S. Army C.I.C. Supervised troop education in Panama.

PERSONAL REFERENCES

Dr. Steven M. Grayson, Director, Head Start, 1211 Peachtree, Atlanta, Georgia
Mr. Warren Franklin, 409 Water Lane, Decatur, Georgia

Sample Resume Critique Form

(A blank form like this for you to copy is given on page 75.)

Resume of Ms. Becky Conway

Item	Score 1	2	3	How It Could Be Improved
1 Overall appearance. Do you want to read it?			X	
2 Layout. Does the resume look professional, well typed and printed, good margins, etc. Do key sales points stand out?		X		Could better highlight sales points.
3 Length. Could the resume tell the same story if it were shortened?		X		The part on education should be shortened, and *Employment* expanded to show accomplishments.
4 Relevance. Has extraneous material been eliminated?	X			Early education, personal statistics, and references should be deleted.
5 Writing Style. Is it easy to get a picture of the applicant's qualifications?	X			Increase the coverage of qualifications—convey more benefits. Eliminate "I have" phrases.
6 Action Orientation. Do sentences and paragraphs begin wih action verbs?	X			Sentences could be more directed to achievement and action—eliminate wind-up phrases.
7 Specificity. Does resume avoid generalities and focus on specific information about experience, projects, products, etc.?		X		Could point out the "quantities"—number of parents counseled, number of books handled.
8 Accomplishments. Are applicant's accomplishments and problem-solving skills emphasized?	X			Applicant's accomplishments are not emphasized.

| 9 Completeness. Is all important information covered? | X | | | What did she do from 1961–66? She forgot zip codes. |
| 10 Bottom Line. How well does the resume accomplish its ultimate purpose of getting the employer to invite the applicant in for an interview? | X | | | The applicant tells us very little about her skills, what she can do and what she has accomplished. She should expand the description of her work experience. |

Rating Point Total 15 (Out of a maximum of 30)

What are some other ways that you would suggest to improve this resume?

The section on employment history should be expanded to twice its size, with a well-written description of accomplishments. This could precede the education section to make it more prominent.

Now It's Your Turn

How did your rating compare with ours? Were you more lenient? Less? Did you suggest some specific areas of improvement? Before you read any more of this chapter, critique your *own* resume. Use another copy of the Resume Critique Form on page 75 of this manual.

Test Marketing Your Resume

How did you do? Were you surprised by your rating? Were you strict with yourself? Did you discover any areas that could be improved?

Take some time now to make any necessary revisions. If you think you need a new draft, prepare one. Then you'll be ready to test market your resume, keeping in mind these few pointers that will help you obtain an objective resume critique:

- If possible, select someone to review your resume who has had some experience in the business or professional world. It could be a friend of a friend, a placement counselor, or a prior employer. Don't be afraid to ask for the kind of help you want and need.

- Phrase your questions to this individual so as to encourage ideas for improvement: "Would you mind looking over this resume and giving me some ideas about how I can make it better?" When you just ask people for an opinion, they are often afraid of being too critical and won't make concrete corrections or suggestions.

- Have the person read your resume once or twice and then put it down; ask that person to describe what he or she has learned about you. If you do this with someone who doesn't know you too well, the feedback you get will reflect the overall impression created by your resume.

- After you have elicited some general comments from the reader, you may wish to focus on specific questions. Ask:

  Do you think my resume should be shortened?
  How would you improve the layout?
  Do I give enough information about my most recent position?
  Is the presentation clear? Compelling?

You can provide each of your critics with one of your copies of the Resume Critique Form if you wish.

Final Touches

After you've had your resume critiqued, use all the information and advice you've gathered to make your final revisions. The next step is to have your completed resume typed and printed. Here are some tips:

- Use a top-quality typewriter with a clean ribbon. If you don't have access to a good typewriter, pay a commercial

service to do the final typing. Have someone, in addition to yourself, proofread for typing errors.
- Take the typed and proofread version of your resume to an established offset printer. (Check your local Yellow Pages.) Have 100 copies printed on a good (but not extravagant) grade of paper. The cost is nominal when you consider the benefits of a well-done resume. Keep the typed original in a sealed flat envelope for possible reprinting.

Now you've done it! It took a lot of time and effort, but what you have created is a document that sets you apart from the crowd and gives you the maximum chance for getting the interviews you want.

We really could close the discussion of resumes here and wish you the best of luck. But first, there's one other item you ought to know about—the cover letter that you must mail along with your resume. This letter is one of the most important pieces of material you'll ever write about yourself.

8 WRITING YOUR COVER LETTERS

SOME PEOPLE LIKE to have more than one resume so that they can emphasize different areas of their expertise and focus each resume on a special job target. However, you probably won't need more than a single version of your current resume if you learn to write a good customized cover letter. Since a cover letter is the ideal place to focus on the specific skills you want to emphasize for a particular employer, a new, individual cover letter must accompany each resume you send out.

A cover letter represents another important opportunity for you; it's like a personal introduction to the employer. A well-written letter will win you important points toward getting your interview.

Here are some guidelines for writing a good cover letter:

- Every resume should be accompanied by an *individualized typed* letter. The objective of the letter is to pinpoint how your skills and experience relate to the particular needs of the employer to whom you're writing. This letter should be addressed specifically to the person—by name and title—who will most likely be doing the interviewing for the job you have in mind. You can generally find out this information by calling the employer's switchboard. (If you are answering a blind newspaper advertisement—one in which the employer is not specified—you can address your letter "To whom it may concern.")

- Each cover letter you write will have a somewhat different slant, depending on what skills are important to the needs of the particular employer. Whenever possible, do some research on the organization or company before you write your cover letter. This research, which is an essential part of every job campaign, can be accomplished by reading annual reports or product brochures, by contacting people in the organization, or, if you have an understanding of the field, simply by asking yourself what kinds of problems this particular employer is likely to be facing.

- Your cover letter should not normally run more than three or four paragraphs and should rarely be more than a page.

- Always close your cover letter with a request for an interview. Suggest a specific time or reason, such as:

  - "I will be in your area next week, and would appreciate the opportunity for an interview on Tuesday or Wednesday."

  - I would like to stop by with some samples of my work in this area. Could we meet briefly next Thursday afternoon?"

  - "I will call your office to discuss a possible interview date."

As you prepare your cover letters, keep in mind the rules of good writing and typing. Make your letters as concise, to the point, and interesting as possible. Remember that they will be viewed as samples of your writing skills.

Sending Out Your Resume

Every time you mail a resume and cover letter, be sure to make a record of it. As you really get into an active job campaign, you'll find it helpful to have names, dates, and schedules for follow-ups, etc., in a convenient place.

On page 83 of this book we've provided a sample Resume

Resume Control Sheet

Resume and Cover Letter Sent to: Name/Address of Organization	Person Sent to and Phone No.	Date	Contact Source	Follow-up Scheduled for:	Initial Response, Comments, Follow-up Strategy

Control Sheet that you can copy and use to record the details you will need. Make additional copies of this form as necessary.

Be sure to make a carbon copy of each cover letter you send out. Keep them all in a file folder for your future reference.

On the following pages are some examples of good resume cover letters.

Sample Cover Letter

415 High Street
Portland, Oregon 97201
Phone: (206) 555–4183
March 28, 1980

Dr. Warren Slaton, President
Seattle Community College
12 Rocky Mount Road
Seattle, Washington 98101

Dear Dr. Slaton:

My experience on the administrative staffs of two colleges should be of interest to you in your new drive to centralize administrative functions of SCC.

The enclosed resume will illustrate my ability to handle the specific administrative problems of a college department.

I am moving to Seattle at the end of this school year. I will be in Seattle April 10–14. If possible, I would like to arrange an appointment during that period to discuss your new organization, and how my experience could make a contribution to your program.

Yours very truly,

Roberta Simon

Enc: Resume

Sample Cover Letter

125 West 89th Street
New York, New York 10024
(212) 555–3878
September 23, 1979

Mrs. Janice Maelson
Staff Director
Urban Renewal Agency
1717 Bronx Park E.
New York, New York 10046

Dear Mrs. Maelson:

Thank you for the time on the telephone yesterday.

I was very interested to hear that you have made so much progress on your relocation study, and that you have already obtained full funding. You have certainly accomplished a lot since we first met at the City Council meeting last year.

After our conversation, I looked up the two reports which you mentioned, and am now more certain than ever that my experience will dovetail nicely with your plans, particularly in the research and report writing phases. As you will note from my resume, I have had a good combination of administrative, research, and writing experience—something that you stated you were looking for.

Although I have received a good offer from a firm in Boston, I would prefer to remain in New York and so would like to meet with you at your earliest convenience—if possible, before the end of the month. Would next Thursday or Friday be good for you? I'll call to find out.

Thank you again for your initial interest. I am looking forward to our getting together so that I can show you some of my work.

Very truly yours,

Alice Hunt

Sample Cover Letter

1736 D Street N.W.
Washington, D.C. 20006
(202) 555–8192

December 28, 1979

Mr. Edward Major, President
Vendo Corporation
1742 Surf Drive
Fort Lauderdale, Florida

Dear Mr. Major:

I was intrigued by the write-up of your new portable vending centers as described in *Sales Management* magazine. Frankly, I think it is an extremely good idea.

As you will note from the enclosed resume, my market planning and sales management experience could be of great assistance to you at this early stage in your project.

Because of my familiarity with the types of locations and clients you are seeking, I am sure that if we were able to work together in this new venture, the results would reflect my contribution.

I have roughed out some specific marketing ideas which you might like to review, and would like to make arrangements to meet with you in Florida during the week of February 15th.

I am looking forward to meeting with you.

Very truly yours,

Jane Hardwick

Congratulations!

You have completed the resume preparation part of this book; we hope you've enjoyed the step-by-step process of writing your resume.

And we hope you've learned a lot more in these pages than just how to write a good resume. Through the self-examination exercises, we've tried to make you aware of your accomplishments and their value in the marketplace. And we wanted you to see that you can increase your value by being willing to contribute your skills to potential employers in ways that fulfill their needs as well as your own.

Having a positive attitude about wanting to contribute value to a potential employer is one of the greatest assets you can have—in your resume and in the interviews to come. That, and the resume you now have, will take you farther than you can imagine.

Good luck in your job search! You are well on your way to getting the interviews you want.

part two

INTERVIEWING TO GET THE JOB YOU WANT

Introduction

It's 9:00 A.M. Margaret Peters is nervous today. Why? Her interview for a position as accountant/bookkeeper at Good Samaritan Hospital is scheduled for 11:00 A.M. This will be her first real job interview. Although she has worked before, she didn't have to interview for the job. When she started college, her Uncle Jim gave her a job as a cashier at one of his three restaurants. Over the next eight years she worked part-time and was trained as a bookkeeper there. By the time she quit, she had not only taken on the responsibility of handling the account books for all his restaurants, she had also completed three years of college. Recently divorced, Margaret now needs to work full-time, and she really wants *this* job. She heard about the opening through her good friend Jan, a nurse at Good Samaritan.

Her mind races. What should I wear? What time should I leave? What happens if the baby-sitter (Jimmy, 6, is home sick from school today) doesn't show up? What do I say when I get there? And how can I stop being so nervous?

Margaret needs more than someone to tell her to relax. She needs a method for controlling her anxiety, and for controlling the interview. By learning the techniques of successful interviewing she will come to realize that her "nervous energy" is commonplace and natural—even desirable, if channeled through the proper outlets. This section of the book has been designed to demonstrate that method and the techniques of successful interviewing. Whether the interview you are preparing for is your first or your fiftieth, the principles in this book will help you.

As a "typical" full-time employee, you will work about 2,000 hours a year (based on fifty 40-hour weeks). If you multiply those 2,000 hours by the number of years you will work, you can see that you are planning for a large percentage of your life (60 *thousand* hours of work in 30 years). To make the most of all those hours and days, you need to land a job that maximizes your potential. *Since nearly 99 percent of employers use the interview to help select and evaluate future employees, it is virtually impossible to land that job without being interviewed for it first.* (The remaining 1 percent hire on the basis of test scores and resumes.) In addition, you will quickly discover that it is often the person who makes the best first impression and is the most skilled at job finding who gets the job, not necessarily the one who is the best qualified.

To help you learn the interviewing skills to be successful, we spoke with all kinds of interviewing experts—professional interviewers and seasoned interviewees, recruiters, personnel officers, management authorities, career developers, employment specialists, and women's career advisors. You will learn from them the techniques that have worked for others, resulting in real job offers. You will also read about mistakes people make and find out how to avoid making them yourself. Throughout the book these experts will give you their hints and inside advice. Among those we would particularly like to thank are Richard Bolles, author of *What Color Is Your Parachute?;* Sharon Bermon, of Counseling Women, New York, N.Y.; Tom Jackson, of Employment Training Corporation, author of *28 Days to a Better Job;* Linda Kline, of Maximus Consulting, Inc., New York, N.Y.; Anita Lands, formerly of our Catalyst staff and now Director of the East Coast Office of the National Association of Bank Women, New York, N.Y.; and Adele Ribolow, of Choices, New York, N.Y.

When we surveyed corporate officials about the interview process, we heard some disturbing comments:

- "I interviewed a woman yesterday who didn't know the first thing about this industry."

- "You wouldn't believe how defensive the interviewee was; she kept apologizing for not having worked before."
- "The woman who was to be interviewed really looked terrific, but it was as if she had dressed for a party. I couldn't possibly send her on to another department for an interview."

By following our guidelines, you can avoid the mistakes these women made. Your interviewers should then sound like this one: "I am really impressed with the women I have been interviewing. I find that they take themselves and their work very seriously; they have a professional attitude."

Before You Begin . . .

The key word in this manual is preparation. As Margaret Peters, our hypothetical job applicant, is discovering, looking for a job is a very serious business. Don't expect to read this book and get the first job for which you interview. Do expect to spend hours of your time—in preparation for, and follow-up after, *every* interview—time very well invested in your career. *You* are your most valuable commodity in terms of your potential earnings and self-fulfillment. As Tom Jackson, the employment specialist, says, "Interviews are not to be treated lightly."

To help you meet the challenge of good, successful interviewing, we provide information covering two areas of preparation. First we deal with the general preparation needed for all interviews; then, in Chapter 4, we tell you how to prepare for *each* particular job opening.

A word to the wise: As you use this guide to help launch your successful interview campaign, remember the words of one recruiter who told us that "I am realistic enough to know that I can't hire someone perfect. No one is perfect." But you can have better interviews, ones that lead to jobs you want. So get started!

1 THE INTERVIEW AND THE INTERVIEWER

On her way to the interview, Margaret has trouble finding the hospital and arrives ten minutes late. (There was a parking lot close by, but to avoid the added expense, she waited for a spot on the street.) Once inside the building, Margaret searches for the comptroller's office. Staring at a vending machine in the corridor wishing she had had another cup of coffee this morning, she begins to have more doubts. "Maybe this is not such a good idea." "Why didn't I just continue to work for my uncle?" "Can I really handle a new job?" But she starts to relax after she finds the right office and meets her interviewer, Mr. Brown. He extends his right hand for shaking, but Margaret is too busy shifting handbag, coat, and by-now limp and dog-eared resume to respond with anything but a mumbled "Hi." Outgoing and pleasant, Mr. Brown quickly puts her at ease, however. When Margaret finally gets settled, she takes out a cigarette. Just as she is about to light it, her eye catches the prominent "No Smoking" sign behind the desk.

A job interview is simply a meeting between an employer and a potential employee. According to the dictionary, "to interview" literally means "to see each other mutually." *Thus, a job interview should be a mutual exploration, with the objective of seeing if a good match exists.* If you ignore the two-sided aspect of the interview and view it, instead, as an inquisition, or even as something that is all-important, ignoring other aspects of landing a job, you will remain intimidated and nervous. *A first step is to consider the interview as an opportunity for interviewer and interviewee to exchange information mutually so that they can both decide if a possible good match can be made.*

As the interviewee, you have two goals. First, you are there to decide whether the position is right for you. Second, at the same time you are conveying the message: "Hire me!" Normally, you will have about 20 to 40 minutes to achieve both these goals. Consider the effects of the powerful psychological difference that exists between an interview that is approached with these goals and the interview that is approached with the *traditional* goal: "I must get this job."

Interviewers, on the other hand, have their own goal: to find out if you are the right person for the position. They must ask themselves such questions as "What can she do for me," "How much will I have to pay," and "Will she fit in here?"

The interviewer is the link between you and the company. When you participate in the interview, you become one side of a triangle, each side of which has its own needs and expectations. In Margaret's case the triangle might be:

Interviewer: Mr. Brown

- Represents the comptroller's department, through that department the personnel department, *and* the administrative position of the hospital
- Wants a good accountant
- Needs someone who will fit in with the current structure

Employer: Good Samaritan Hospital

- Has responsibility to the community
- Hopes to get job done well, but at least cost
- Must maintain its image

EMPLOYER — INTERVIEWER — INTERVIEWEE

Interviewee: Margaret

- Wants the job
- Needs the salary
- Wants to further career goals

Remember, interviews are stressful situations for both you *and* your interviewer. Richard Bolles in *What Color Is Your Parachute?* tells us that "in one twenty-minute interview . . . the man [or the woman] with the power to hire can botch up part of the organization, cost the organization a great deal of money, lose his or her own promotion, be called to account, and acquire a whole new set of ulcers. No wonder hiring is such a stressful situation."*

One excellent way of significantly cutting down on stress is to be prepared. Both interviewers and interviewees do their jobs better when they come prepared. In fact, just as this manual is for interviewees, many books have been written expressly for the interviewer. Two of the most widely used interviewing manuals are *The Evaluation Interview,* by Richard A. Fear (New York: McGraw-Hill, 1972) and *The Interviewer's Manual,* by Henry H. Morgan and John W. Cogger (New York: The Psychological Corporation, 1973).

Put Yourself in the Interviewer's Place

If you familiarize yourself with the general rules for interviewers, you will know some of the "whys" behind the questions you as interviewee will be asked. This insider's knowledge of the interviewer's objectives should help to lessen your on-the-spot apprehension.

The interviewer should understand the actual job requirements and what the job demands; plus the training requirements, salary, and working conditions. For example:

- What physical requirements must the job holder fulfill (the energy, strength, stamina, and skills needed)?
- What are the mental tasks that the job holder must perform (the talents, skills, and knowledge required)?

What Color Is Your Parachute?, by Richard Nelson Bolles (Berkeley, California: Ten Speed Press, 1977), p. 144.

- What are the incentives for the job (the rewards and satisfactions that result from doing the job)?
- What are the social, political, and ethical demands (the groups and issues or principles associated with doing the job)?
- What are the hazards or disadvantages (the dangers, risks, and pressures that accompany the job)?

The interviewer should become thoroughly acquainted with the candidate by carefully reviewing the application and resume before the interview, and during the interview by following a specific format (known as a structured interview) that explores the following areas: work experience, education and training, outside activities and interests, and early years. The interviewer should try to discover information about the person's personality and her social, communicative, analytical, and decision-making skills.

The interviewer should use questions designed to get the information needed. He or she should probe when necessary for verification and clarity. Three common types of questions may be used:

- Open-ended questions, those questions used to draw out the applicant ("Tell me about your previous job experience").
- Closed questions, those questions used to control the interview; these questions do not allow the interviewee to give much information ("So, you worked in an office before").
- Probing questions, those questions used to elicit a clearer response ("What did you mean when you said . . . ?").

The interviewer should present the job and the organization positively and accurately; if there are special conditions (such as the need to share work space or work overtime), they should be clearly stated.

Also, the interviewer should allow the applicant to talk about 75 percent of the time. Several interviewers told us that they really appreciate the interviewee who talks and asks questions. As one interviewer said, "When that happens, I don't have to work so hard." Interestingly, research shows that interviewers actually talk about 65 percent of the time, and applicants only 35 percent.

The excerpt from *The Interviewer's Manual* that appears at the end of this chapter gives a good example of the general areas covered by the interviewer and the types of questions used in a structured interview. Most often, interviewers are encouraged to conduct a *structured* interview using a specific format, such as the interview guide on page 106, to be used with all interviewees. The summary section of the interview guide on page 108 shows how a professional interviewer evaluates an interview. The references to zero prejudice (EEO) allows the interviewer to factor in prejudices and to try to negate their influence. In an *unstructured* interview the questions follow no particular order and are often "spontaneous."

What Impresses Interviewers?

Obviously, every interviewer you meet will be different; some will be better at interviewing than others. But each will have a unique personality and come equipped with personal likes and dislikes. Interviewers are encouraged to put their personal biases aside, but that, as we know, is easier to preach than practice. Nevertheless, there are some factors that most impress interviewers.

In general, interviewers make their decisions on the basis of appearance, perceived or demonstrated motivation, communication skills, academic standing (particularly with recent graduates), and personality. Not surprisingly, command of speech is often used as a way of "measuring" intelligence and competence, particularly for managerial and executive positions.

Some other very important points:

• Interviewers develop stereotypes of good candidates and

seek to match people with these stereotypes (which are often similar to themselves).

- Interviewers are more influenced by *un*favorable information than by favorable information.
- Interviewers make their overall evaluation of the candidate within the first four minutes of the interview. *(Contact: The First Four Minutes,* by Leonard Zunin, M.D., and Natalie Zunin (New York: Ballantine, 1972), investigates this "four-minute barrier" in all new relationships.)

The following report summarizes the advice given by campus recruiters to job-seeking students; it is reprinted with permission of the Columbia University Graduate School of Business.

A Report from Recruiters to Students

A. What Turns On Recruiters at On-Campus Interviews

1. Evidence of self-analysis—you know why you're in the interview.
2. Evidence that you take the interview seriously, as demonstrated by being well prepared for it.
3. Enthusiasm.
4. Recognition that interviewing is a difficult process.

B. Qualities Recruiters Are Looking For

1. GENERAL: See your boy/girl scout manual—ambition, poise, sincerity, trustworthiness, articulateness, analytical ability, initiative, interest in the firm. (Overall general intelligence is assumed because you're here, believe it or not.) Different firms look for different kinds of people— personalities, style, appearance, abilities, and technical skills. Always check the posted job specs for any interview, and don't waste time talking about a job you can't

do or for which you don't have the minimum qualifications.

2. DRESS: Look like a businessperson unless there's a sensible extenuating circumstance—DO EXPLAIN. Be neat and clean. Don't be sloppy. Don't dress in extreme ways.

3. GRADES: The importance of grades varies from firm to firm. For some they're critical, for others unimportant. Be sure to check job specs posted. Be able to explain marked deficiencies, if asked. On-campus interviewers don't know your grades in advance but are likely to ask you about them. They *may* ask you to release your transcript. They *may* ask you for the name of a faculty reference of *your* choice or they *may* later inquire about you from a faculty member whom *they* know personally.

4. EXPERIENCE: Again, this varies from job to job. Check posted specifications. "Two years' experience" means you have to have a *minimum of two years' experience!* If you've had work experience, be able to articulate the importance of what you did in terms of the job for which you are interviewing and in terms of your own growth or learning.

5. KNOWLEDGE OF THE RECRUITER'S COMPANY AND INDUSTRY: At a *minimum,* you really *are* expected to have read everything the company has put in the placement library. Don't waste interview time by asking questions you could have had answered by the printed material. Know the firm's position and character relative to others in the same industry. General awareness of media coverage of a firm and its industry is usually expected.

What Does Not Impress Interviewers?

The Columbia Graduate School of Business gives us these three categories of "turnoffs":

1. Lack of preparation (this gives evidence of noninterest).

2. Inappropriate qualifications for positions the firm is seeking to fill, as noted in the placement office job listings.
3. Overconfidence, cockiness, put-ons, falseness, superficiality, and late arrival.

Several experts cited the first "turnoff," lack of preparation, as particularly bothersome to interviewers. Tom Jackson comments: "The traditional mistake of an interviewee is not being prepared. That is stupid. Think of the interview as a demonstration kit; you are demonstrating how you would get the job done. Being unprepared at the interview tells the interviewer that you are the kind of person who would probably go into meetings unprepared."

In this case, the medium really is the message. This is your chance, using the interview as the medium, to project the message: *This is how I would get the job done; you should hire me!*

General Tips

Although this guide is geared toward the typical interview used to decide on employment, the *hiring* interview, you may adapt its principles for a variety of situations. Another type of interview that has become increasingly popular is the *information* interview, described by Richard Bolles in *What Color Is Your Parachute?* In this case *you* conduct the interview to learn more about the job or industry in which you are interested. You approach the company as an information seeker, rather than as a job seeker. This approach gives the applicant more control and, according to Bolles, makes the job and the information seeker feel "less like a victim" (unfortunately, some people do feel victimized by the standard interview process).

Remember, hiring interviews as well as information interviews should be learning experiences. No one expects you to land your first job at your first interview. Don't let bad experiences stop you. Use each interview to learn about yourself and various industries and positions. According to Tom Jackson, "A new game starts with every interview. If you had six interviews that didn't work, don't look at the seventh as one of seven; think of it as the first one. Don't think of yourself as being on a losing streak."

Start fresh with each interview, but *don't start until you are ready*. If you have not thought about your skills and needs, if you have no idea what kind of job you want, you should not be going out on interviews.

Test Yourself: How Would You Handle This Situation?

Lee S. has been working at a magazine for only six months as an editorial assistant. She has not bothered to update her resume. At 11:00 AM her friend Kathy calls to tell her of a terrific opening at a movie production company. Kathy knows the producer, Tom, and he is expecting Lee's call. Lee arranges for a 12:30 appointment and she rushes off. In the waiting room, she neatly adds information about her present job to her old resume. (She retrieved one from the personnel office of her employer, the magazine.)

When the interview begins, Lee and Tom enthusiastically converse until she hands him her resume. After he sees it, he thanks her politely, but his attitude has definitely changed. Kathy calls her around 4:00 to report: "Tom really liked you but he figured if you cared so little about yourself that you would write all over your resume, you couldn't take your work very seriously. He thinks you would probably send out sloppy reports and letters."

Lee was mortified! She was known for her careful attention to details. She had assumed that Tom would rather have a resume with handwritten additions than an out-of-date one. The crucial word here is *assumed*. The message Tom picked up was exactly the opposite of what Lee was trying to convey.

What should Lee have done? One general rule: Whenever there are unusual or special circumstances, be sure to explain: "As you know, we just made this appointment today. I will send my resume to you tomorrow by messenger" (then redo it that evening) or, "Here is a copy of my resume. As you can see, it is not up-to-date. I wasn't looking for another position, but this sounded like a terrific opportunity. Shall I fill in my experience for you?" Another possibility would have been for Lee to call and ask to see Tom again or to have explained the circumstances in a follow-up letter.

Structure your responses to fit your own style and needs. Remember, always ask yourself, "What message am I conveying?"

How Can You Avoid Margaret's Mistakes?

1. Allow extra time to cope with unexpected occurrences. Starting late is starting with a strike against you.
2. Preparation, even with regard to such things as what you are going to wear, will make you feel more relaxed, less harried, on the morning of the interview. A *good* night's sleep is necessary (and as much coffee as you normally require in the morning) to appear as alert and responsive as you can.
3. If you're running late and it's absolutely unavoidable, call the interviewer to let him or her know; the interviewer might prefer to reschedule your appointment. Showing up late without calling first can cost you the job no matter how qualified you are.
4. Ask for clear instructions on how to get to the place of the interview, and where to park if necessary.
5. Consider taking public transportation if possible, so that you will have more time to relax and collect your thoughts.
6. If you drive and parking is a problem, spend the few extra dollars it costs to park in a lot. It may save you from arriving late or getting needlessly flustered.
7. If possible, leave all unnecessary things like your coat or extra bag in the outer office. Ask the receptionist or secretary for assistance. That way your hands will be free, and you'll look more in charge. A good *firm* handshake is in order if the interviewer offers a hand.

8. Keep your extra resume in a place where it will remain unsmudged and uncrumpled (a stiff file folder or briefcase—not loose in your hand, which is apt to be shaky and damp).

9. "Hi" is O.K. for your friends, but when meeting an interviewer it's definitely not in order. "How do you do" or "hello" is best, taking your cues from the interviewer's greeting.

10. Don't smoke at the interview unless your interviewer clearly offers you a cigarette. Even then, it may be best to wait until the interview is over so that your hands are free (preferably kept relaxed in your lap).

Some Evaluations Your Interviewer Is Making During the Interview

- How mentally alert and responsive is the applicant?
- How well does the applicant follow the interviewer's train of thought?
- Is the applicant able to draw proper inferences and conclusions during the course of the interview?
- Does the applicant demonstrate a degree of intellectual depth in her conversation or does she appear to be shallow or superficial in her thinking?
- Has she used good judgment and common sense in the way she has planned and led her life so far?
- Does she appear able to think and respond spontaneously?
- What is the applicant's capacity for problem-solving activities?
- Is she excessively self-centered, or is she capable of identifying with her company's goals and objectives?
- How well does the candidate respond to stress and pressure or the opposite?*

*Excerpted by permission of the publisher from *Successful Personnel Recruiting and Selection,* by Erwin S. Stanton, © 1977 by AMACOM, a division of American Management Associations. All rights reserved.

Interview Guide

LISTEN

Be Receptive
and Responsive

COMMENT

Make
Conversation

INQUIRE

Probe: What?
How?
Why?

Keep Questions Open-Ended
Use Plural and Contrast Questions
Rephrase "YES/NO"—Restate More Fully

INTRODUCTION

Cover:
Greeting
Small talk
Opening question
Lead question

Look for:
Appearance
Manner
Self-expression
Responsiveness

WORK EXPERIENCE

Cover:
Earliest jobs:
 part-time, temporary
 Military assignments
 Full-time positions
 Volunteer work

Ask:
Things done best? Done less well?
Things liked best? Liked less well?
Major accomplishments? How achieved?
Most difficult problems faced? How handled?
Ways most effective with people? Ways less effective?
Reasons for changing jobs?
What learned from work experience?
What looking for in job? In career?
Short-term and long-range goals?

Look for:
Relevance of work
Sufficiency of work
Skill and competence
Adaptability
Productivity
Motivation
Interpersonal relations
Leadership
Growth and development

EDUCATION

Cover:
(Elementary school)
High school
College
Specialized training
Recent courses

Ask:
Best subjects? Subjects done less well?
Subjects liked most? Liked least?
Reactions to teachers?
Level of grades? Effort required?
Reasons for choosing school? Major field?
Special achievements? Toughest problems?
Role in extracurricular activities?
How financed education?
Relation of education to career?
Consider further schooling or specialized training?

Look for:
Relevance of schooling
Sufficiency of schooling
Intellectual abilities
Versatility
Breadth and depth of
 knowledge
Level of accomplishment
Motivation, interests
Reaction to authority
Leadership
Teamwork

PRESENT ACTIVITIES AND INTERESTS *(optional)* *

Cover:

Special interests and hobbies
Civic and community affairs that are job relevant
Health and energy
Geographical preferences

Ask:

Things like to do in spare time?
Extent involved in community?

What kind of health problems might affect job performance?
Reaction to relocation? to travel?
Circumstances that might influence job performance?

Look for:

Vitality
Management of time, energy, money
Maturity and judgment
Intellectual growth
Cultural breadth
Diversity of interests
Social effectiveness
Interpersonal skills and interests
Leadership
Basic values and goals
Situational factors

SUMMARY

Cover:

Strengths (Assets)

Ask:

What bring to job? What are assets?

What are best talents?

What qualities seen by self or others?
What makes you good investment for employer?

Look for:

PLUS (+)
AND MINUS (−)
Can do?
Talents, skills
Knowledge
Energy

Cover:
Shortcomings
(Development needs)

Ask:
What are some shortcomings or limitations?
What areas need improvement?
What qualities wish to develop further?
What constructive criticism from others?
How might be a risk for employer?
What further training, or experience, might need?

Will do?
Motivation
Interests

How fit?
Personal qualities
Social effectiveness
Character

Situational factors

Synthesis

Zero prejudice (EEO)

CLOSING REMARKS (Adapt to context)

Cover:
Dialogue: give information
Review job and opportunities; sell, if appropriate
Further contacts to be made
Course of action to be taken

CORDIAL PARTING (Spontaneous)

*NOTE: Personal information is *optional* and should be *job relevant.*

Job Hint #1

"If you have always wanted a job with Avon, don't interview there first. Take some 'throw away' interviews. You will be more comfortable. And as the comfort level goes up, you do better."

—Linda Kline
Maximus Consulting, Inc.
New York, N.Y.

Job Hint #2

"If you don't know what you want to do, for heaven's sake don't interview for a job right now. Take 2 weeks or 2 months and schedule interviews with people who are working at jobs you might want. Apart from the information you obtain about yourself and the job market, interviewing for information about jobs, rather than asking for jobs you don't want and which might not be available, is a surefire way to become comfortable in the interviewing game."

—Richard K. Irish
TransCentury Corp.
Washington, D.C.

2 GETTING READY

(Back at the interview with Mr. Brown) As Margaret reluctantly puts away her cigarette, she apologizes for being late. After a brief but awkward moment or two, Mr. Brown explains the responsibilities for the junior accountant position. Margaret seems to have no questions. "Do you think you can handle this job?" Mr. Brown asks. "Sure," responds Margaret, "I have done this sort of thing before." A long pause follows. Mr. Brown clears his throat and continues again: "What things do you enjoy, Margaret? What are you good at?" Margaret stares at him perplexed. "What am I really good at?" she wonders. "And what does Mr. Brown want to hear?" She stammers, "Oh . . . uh . . . well, I'm good at lots of things." ("But not at interviewing," she adds mentally as she stares at the floor and waits for the next question.) "I assume you are good at figures," Mr. Brown prompts her patiently. "Of course, I'm a very good bookkeeper," she replies. Mr. Brown nods, hoping she will continue, but Margaret is silent.

There are three golden rules for interviews, in addition to those other golden rules for life in general, as our expert Anita Lands says: Be Yourself; Know Yourself; Sell Yourself. Follow these rules faithfully, and you will be a more successful interviewee.

Golden Rule Number 1: Be Yourself.

Don't make the mistake of trying to "be" someone you are not. Since there is no one perfect applicant for any job, don't try to second-guess your interviewer and try to act like the person you think the interviewer wants you to be.

Many people mistakingly "leave" their real personalities outside the interviewer's door. They submerge their natural enthusiasm and act overly stiff and distant. One interviewer recalls her experience hiring a librarian: She interviewed twenty people in a short period, and, as she says, "So many of the applicants acted like robots. It was refreshing to meet anyone who seemed real. As it turned out I hired the one qualified person who acted the most like a real librarian would be on the job—rather relaxed and natural, not false or posing (of course, her experience and credentials were good too, but her natural manner really clinched it for me)."

Golden Rule Number 2: Know Yourself.

Before anyone else can get to know you, you must know yourself. Know what you like to do and are good at before you are questioned by someone else. Thoughtful self-analysis should include answers to the following questions:

- What are your strengths and weaknesses, abilities, talents, interests, likes and dislikes, needs, values, accomplishments, prior work experiences, future job expectations, short-, medium- and long-term goals, your (and your partner's) future plans? (The answers to many of these questions may have been discovered when you went through a career options exploration or when you prepared your resume.)
- Do you prefer people- or data-oriented tasks?
- Can you tolerate working under pressure or do you desire very relaxed working conditions?
- What have you gained from your past experience? How would it apply to the job you want?
- How would you describe yourself?

Don't underestimate the need to put yourself through this kind of personal third degree. Listen to the experts: Over and over interviewers told us they hire people who know themselves and their skills. As one recruiter put it, "I hire people who are realistic about themselves, and who can rate (and discuss) their successes and failures."

Golden Rule Number 3: Sell Yourself.

A good salesperson is someone who has done her homework and who knows the product's strengths and weaknesses. In this case *you* are the product. If you don't believe in you—what you have to offer—why should anyone else? Some people have trouble expressing their positive qualities; they may be self-conscious about pushing themselves or blowing their own horn, so to speak. But it's very important to be able to communicate your skills and qualities that will help the interviewer evaluate your ability to do the job. Some women may need special coaching in this aspect of selling themselves. If you feel you need to learn to be more assertive, try one of the many courses and counseling services designed for this purpose. It will pay off when interviewing for the job you want.

Now that you know the three golden rules for interviewing, you can start to work on preparing for the interview itself. In a successful interview you must relate your skills to the employer's needs. But before you can do that you must know the following three things:

- Your skills
- The employer
- The demands of the position

Knowing Your Skills

You have more skills than you think! Most people don't realize all the skills they have. To help you get to know what all your skills are, go back to page 37 in the resume preparation section of this book. Do the skills assessment exercise again. As you go through the list, feel free to add other skills—your own or ones you'd like to have or think are important. Check whether you think you are excellent, very good, or good, and comment on the skills listed. As a means of jogging your memory, give an example of how you have used each skill. This exercise will help you in the interview. Remember: It doesn't matter where or how you learned or developed the skill—in school, as a result of special training, through volunteer work, or such other methods as observation or life experience.

Character Traits

Another way of stimulating self-analysis is by rating yourself on the following sixteen character traits sought by most employers. Go through the following list (adapted from *So You're Looking for a Job?,* College Placement Counsel, Inc., Box 2263, Bethlehem, Pennsylvania 18001). Rate your competence (excellent, very good, good, fair) and give an example for each trait that comes from your own experience.

  Ability to communicate
  Intelligence
  Self-confidence
  Willingness to accept responsibility
  Initiative
  Leadership
  Energy level
  Imagination
  Flexibility
  Interpersonal skills

Self-knowledge
Ability to handle conflict
Competitiveness
Goal achievement
Vocational skills
Direction

Knowing the Employer and the Industry

You should be as familiar with the industry (or industries) you are interested in as you can be. Research each company as you set up an interview. (In Chapter 4 you'll learn how to research a *specific* company.) Most people betray their lack of preparation for the interview (and for considering a job offer) by failing to do this very important step in the interview process. Never go for an interview with the XYZ Company without knowing as much as you possibly can about XYZ and companies like it. As Sharon Bermon of Counseling Women says, "We feel so strongly that this kind of preparation is essential that we keep organizational files, company files in alphabetical order, and as many annual reports as we can so that women can consult them for research before interviewing."

If you are doing research on your own, your library is an invaluable tool. Most organizations, and the corresponding industries, are listed in some sort of directory, available in a library near you. Enlist the help of your librarian to find what you need. If you are interested in a position in business or industry, your primary research can proceed easily with the use of such directories, which list names, addresses, type and size of companies, as well as the names and titles of key executives. Consult Dun and Bradstreet's *Middle Market Directory* and *Million Dollar Directory;* Standard and Poor's *Directory of Directories;* the *National Advertising Register;* and Thomas' *Register of American Manufacturers*. A "super" directory, the *Directory of Directories*, lists and gives addresses for directories in almost every field you can think of—from crafts to industrial engineering, from health care to safety. The *Encyclopedia of*

Associations contains listings for approximately 500 professional associations ranging from career field organizations to not-for-profit groups. And *The Foundation Directory* can help you if you're researching a foundation as a possible employer.

Another handy tool is the *Employer Directory,* which lists employers of all types in cities and towns throughout the United States. If you're interested in education as a career field, you'll want to check available local or regional directories of public schools as well as the books *Private Schools* and *Schools Abroad.* Almost all public libraries keep up-to-date copies of directories and publications of this type. Other specialized references that can be helpful, depending on your career field, are such publications as *Literary Marketplace,* the *Museum Directory,* the *Hospital Directory,* or the *Membership Roster of the American Association of Advertising Agencies.*

Also look for these publications during your research stage of preparing for your interviews:

Guide to American Directories
B. Kline and Company
11 Third Street
Rye, New York 10580

Describes 3,300 directories of nearly 400 topics

Standard Rate and Data Business Publications Directory
Standard R & D Service
5201 Old Orchard Road
Skokie, Illinois 60076

Includes the names and addresses of trade publications in thousands of fields, listed by topic

Encyclopedia of Business Information Sources
Gale Research
Book Tower
Detroit, Michigan 48226

Listings and details of business source books, periodicals, organizations, directories, bibliographies, and handbooks. Includes wide array of other sources of information on major business topics.

The Standard Periodical Directory
Oxbridge Publishing Company, Inc.
40 East 34th Street
New York, New York 10016

Covers thousands of periodicals and directories of over 200 topics.

Knowing the Demands of the Position

The third part of getting ready for interviews involves discovering what the jobs the employer has to offer involve—what they mean in everyday terms. For instance, you cannot expect to successfully interview for a position as a horticulturist or research assistant if you have only a very vague idea of what a horticulturist or research assistant does. For some general information on specific jobs, use your library again. Look up the job titles you need to know about in the *Dictionary of Occupational Titles,* published by the U.S. Department of Labor, or the *Occupational Outlook Handbook,* a standard guidebook. You may discover that you are qualified for many more positions than you previously thought; so don't let those strange-sounding job titles scare you away before you've researched what they really mean. Also, take the advice of our Job Hint #2 mentioned previously: Set up some information interviews with people in the industries (and positions) that interest you to discuss various positions and what they entail in those industries.

When you have finished your research, you will be able to relate your skills to each employer's needs as you get ready for specific interviews. Unlike Margaret, you should have no trouble answering Mr. Brown's questions: What are you good at? What do you like doing? Why did you choose *this* occupation?

How Can You Avoid Margaret's Mistakes?

1. Relax and *Be Yourself*. Some small talk is appropriate when beginning the interview, but be careful not to chatter on for too long. Avoid long silences though. Your interviewer will most likely try to put you at your ease; do the same for him or her.

2. Be prepared to discuss your qualifications and relate your past experience concisely yet fully. *Know Yourself* and what you want to convey. If you have trouble remembering all you've prepared to discuss, write it down and memorize the essential information before the interview.

3. Ask questions that show you are awake and interested in the job. Make eye contact with your interviewer, not the floor. Smile even though it hurts. *Sell Yourself*.

3 GETTING SET

Margaret continues to show her inexperience and lack of preparation at interviewing. . . .

Mr. Brown: Why did you choose bookkeeping, Margaret?

Margaret: When I was 17, I started to work at one of my uncle's restaurants. He taught me how to keep the books. I discovered I was good at it.

Mr. Brown: That's good. But why do you want to work at Good Samaritan Hospital?

Margaret: Well, I need a job. My friend Jan works here, too.

Mr. Brown: What are your immediate goals? Do you have any you'd like to discuss?

Margaret: (TO HERSELF): To survive this interview and these questions. (ALOUD): Yes, Mr. Brown, I do. I want to complete my bachelor's degree in accounting. I have only 18 credits to go.

Mr. Brown: I certainly hope you make it, Ms. Peters. Where are you studying?

A large part of your interview will involve questions—answering them and asking them. This chapter focuses on helping you prepare for the types of questions you are most likely going to be asked. Many of these questions will be general; but when you arrange each specific interview, review it and prepare the particular answers that demonstrate how your skills relate to that employer's needs and show your familiarity with the industry and company. Remember that the fundamental question (although it may not be stated so bluntly *or even directly expressed at all*) is: "Why should I hire you?" And all your answers should in effect say, "You should hire me because . . ." although you may never use those exact words.

Questions, Questions, More Questions

Three General Questions

The ten most common questions asked during interviews are given later in this chapter. But first review and practice answers to the three types of general questions consistently asked in interviews. These questions are open-ended; they can elicit a great deal of information, placing the burden on you, the interviewee, to decide what and how much to say.

Tell me about yourself

First, be prepared to answer the most basic question: "What can you tell me about yourself?" This type of question gives you a chance to show your understanding of the three golden rules— Be Yourself, Know Yourself, and Sell Yourself. For your answer, you may want to quickly cover a few main areas: your growing-up years, your education, work experience, outside activities, etc. Highlight the areas in which you excel. But don't simply recite your resume, since the interviewer has seen that document. And the danger in making your statement too chronological ("I was born in 1944 in Tampa, Florida . . . and then I attended . . .") is that by the time you get to the important facts, the interviewer may be asleep.

The crucial question for you to ask *yourself* when preparing to answer is what would you hate the interviewer *not* to know about you? Then *make sure that you tell him or her that thing first.* For example: "I was just appointed to the Mayor's Health Task Force," "I am a terrific problem solver; at my last job I was able to . . ." Make sure you get across your good points and accomplishments. Again, this kind of question allows you to do a sales job for yourself in a completely acceptable way.

Avoid being vague. Two statements about yourself that are guaranteed to get you nowhere are: "I want to work with people" and "I want to do something that fulfills me." Although these two goals are fine and even admirable, they really don't tell interviewers anything specific, and chances are they've heard them too many times to care. To help organize your answer, use an index card to write down the four or five things about yourself that you want the employer to know. Review them before each interview.

What Don't You Want Me to Ask You About?

You will probably never be asked the flip side of the "tell me about yourself" question directly, but you must be prepared for it: "What don't you want to talk about?" The question may not be phrased this way, but may be a part of the interview. To prepare, analyze your problem areas. Review your resume and ask yourself honestly whether there are any obvious gaps in employment. Have you ever switched jobs or fields? Often? Have you moved a lot? Were you ever out of work for extended periods? The experts suggest that if there is such an obvious "weakness" in your history, *you* should be the one to bring it up so that *you* control the discussion. At the very least, you should be fully prepared to respond. (One interviewer told us that whenever she sees unexplained years in a resume, she begins to imagine the worst. She thinks: Was the interviewee in the hospital, "dropping out," having a nervous breakdown, in prison? The best strategy? Anticipate these types of questions and learn to answer them in work-related terms. Also practice responding directly and winding up on a positive note.

For example, if asked, "Why have you moved so often?" you might respond, "I can understand why you would ask, because it does seem like I have been jumping from place to place, but I do feel I have gained from living in different parts of the country and meeting many people. In fact . . ." (Add as many pluses as you can). If you have been a homemaker for several years, you might want to volunteer that information on a positive note, stressing your good points and stability. You can't deny the fact that you have changed jobs or areas frequently or haven't been employed out of the home for lengthy periods, but you *can* add positive information about those experiences. Don't be apologetic or defensive; be positive and forthright.

List those questions you think you personally might have trouble answering. Everyone has something in her bio that might work against her. Your own weak spots may involve your lack of experience, poor grades, a health-related problem, etc. But don't let it defeat you. Prepare an answer (or initial statement to make if the topic is introduced), and you'll help your interviewer resolve his or her questions, most likely in your favor.

Some Sample Problem Areas and Answers

Make your own list of personal problem areas. Imagine the questions you might be asked and prepare a positive answer or statement of your own. Use the following questions and responses to trigger your thoughts on your own list.

1. Why did you take so long to finish college? It doesn't appear that you were working during that period.

Actually, I was in a car accident in my junior year. It took quite a while before I was able to go back full-time. Except for my slight limp I am totally recovered. It's interesting because the accident gave me time to . . . (A wrong answer would have been: "It wasn't my fault I took so long. I was in an accident. I finished school when I could." or, "What's it to you?"

2. You seem a little young for this position.

I may be slightly younger than many of the people here, but my age does not seem inconsistent with the nature of the job. I know I can bring fresh ideas plus a lot of energy to the job. (A wrong answer might possibly be: "Actually I've been older than I am ever since I can remember.")

3. I see you majored in French. Have you had any business courses?

My liberal arts studies have taught me how to reason and how to approach problems. But my knowledge of business isn't academic — I was business manager of the college newspaper for 2 years and I've worked in offices for 3 summers.

4. Your past experience was in not-for-profit work. Do you know how profitable corporations like this one operate?

I certainly do — I belong to a professional association that offers seminars in business management. And I learned that sound management and careful budgeting are as important in the not-for-profit world as in a company like this one.

5. All your previous work was as a volunteer. Have you ever held a "real" job?

My volunteer work really was a "real" job — I managed personnel and worked within a strict budget, planned programs, analyzed the market for those programs, and implemented and evaluated them.

How Much Money Do You Want?

Another very important kind of question you must consider carefully beforehand concerns money, your salary and benefit package. The experts differ on their advice about money questions. Some advise *you* to bring up the subject; others say wait until your interviewer mentions compensation. They all, however, agree that with jobs having salaries over $20,000, the interviewer should introduce the subject. (In some cases, of course, you will know exactly what the job pays before you interview, particularly if it is being offered through an employment agency or involves a fixed union salary.)

According to Linda Kline, the management consultant, "Women are afraid that if they ask for what they really want, they will be turned down. If a [large] company wants you, $1,000 more or less is not usually going to matter." Asking for too little, on the other hand, may actually hurt you. She explains: "If the job pays $25–30,000, I can't tell them that since you make only $15,000 now, you therefore will take less than $25,000. They will think you are not qualified . . . or that you're crazy." Another counselor told us that "people will ask you what *you* think *you* are worth to try to figure out your level. When I ask a job candidate how much she wants, I am wondering, 'Is this a $10,000 person?' If she says she is making $22,000, I then have to revise my opinion. The quickest way to evaluate someone is to ask her how much she wants."

The other side of the salary question is, "What were you making at your previous job?" Women often make so much less than men that if their salaries are continuously based on that of their previous jobs, they will never break out of the rut. How do you respond to questions about your former salary?

Almost every expert we polled said you should add about 20 to 30 percent to your previous salary when you answer, because the employer assumes you will anyway! Previous salaries are almost never specifically checked by employers except in certain instances; for example, if you apply for a job in the stock market or liquor industry, or for a high-level government position, you might be subject to very close scrutiny, including your salary record. Many people who do add 20 to 30 percent justify the added amount on the basis that they have included the value of their fringe benefits package. For example, if they made $15,000 and had $3,000 more in benefits (health insurance, pension, etc.), they would add that $3,000 more in benefits (20 percent of their salary) and say that the job was worth $18,000.

Job Hint #3

"If you are asked point-blank what you were making in your previous job and it was much lower than you should be getting, and you feel you shouldn't lie, say, 'I don't think what I'm making now is relevant. I have the expertise for this position, and the jobs I have been considering have been in this range.'"

—Linda Kline,
Maximus Consulting, Inc.

Some Final Thoughts About Salary . . .

Many people find negotiating salaries very difficult, but it certainly is a skill well worth learning. At the most basic level, anyone can handle simple salary negotiation. As Richard Bolles says in *What Color Is Your Parachute?*, be sure you ask: "What is the salary likely to be?" and then simply respond very matter-of-factly whether or not it is satisfactory.

The Salary Question In Brief: Try to let the interviewer bring money up first (to state a range). Don't leave the interview without knowing the salary range. One way to ask is to say "What is budgeted for this position?" Know what the job is worth and what you will accept; and if the job pays too little, be prepared to say so. Don't undersell yourself or think you must accept or reject the offer then and there. The actual negotiations will take place when, and if, you are offered the job. And at that time, take your time before committing yourself so that you can make an informed decision that you won't regret.

The Ten Most Common Interview Questions

Prepare yourself to answer the most common questions asked in job interviews. The ten questions given here are representative ones cited as coming up in interview after interview. (After reading the previous discussions, you are already well prepared to answer one of them.) There is no *one* right answer, so prepare an answer that works for you. Someone else's terrific response may be wrong for you. Remember: Know Yourself, Be Yourself, Sell Yourself.

Question 1. What are Your Major Strengths?

Sometimes this question is asked as "What are your major accomplishments?" To answer, analyze the position for which you are applying. Connect your strengths with the specific skills being sought. ("I am an extremely careful, organized person" might be a good response for a research job.) Try to keep your answers related to work skills needed in the job. One personnel manager shared her experiences: "I always make it a point to ask about your best achievements or accomplishments. Often, the answer will depend on how long you have been out of school. One notable accomplishment might be that you graduated from Harvard. One man when asked this question said, 'My two daughters.' It might have sounded phony or corny from someone else, but it wasn't from him. I look at the whole text of your answer.* It's what you consider important."

---

*Unfortunately, this response might not have received such a good reaction if a woman had said it. It was "unexpected" from a man. It's best to relate your achievements to your job.

Question 2. What Are Your Major Weaknesses?

Keep your answer to this question work related. No one wants to hear that you're always on a diet or that you are sloppy. The most common advice given by interviewers is that you should always present what would be considered a strength as a weakness: "I work too hard"; "I am a perfectionist"; "I am very demanding of myself"; etc. As well, point out that the position that you are applying for can help you maximize your *strengths*.

If you feel comfortable and secure at the actual interview, you might want to use this question to *correct* an impression or as a way of showing that you do know yourself. When one applicant answered, "I have a tendency to dominate the conversation, which you probably noticed," the interviewer agreed with her assessment and hired her.

Question 3. How Is Your Previous Experience Applicable to the Work We Do Here?

This question gives you a good chance to look good. You have done your homework and you understand the nature of the company and the position. Relate your experience to the demands of the position. If you are switching careers, you will have to show how your experience is *transferable*. Explain how your previous work and interests qualify you for this new work.

Sharon Bermon suggests that if you are looking for a sales position, for example, you might try: "I'm changing careers after a careful reassessment. I have been teaching but I've discovered that what I have always been really good at is selling. When I was 10, I had a lemonade stand and I loved it. I always sold more than any other kid on the block. And when our school PTA was raising money, I was always the teacher who was asked to call on potential contributors." Stress your successes and *organize* what you are going to say.

Question 4. Why Did You Leave Your Former Job?

This may be one of those potentially difficult questions—in which case you must anticipate it and prepare an appropriate response. If you were laid off for economic reasons, say so: "Yes, in fact, my whole department was laid off"; "My company went bankrupt"; "The firm had to cut back—some of us were let go." If you have been fired, you have several choices. Choose an answer that is truthful and one with which you are comfortable. For example, "I took a job that was really not right for me, and I should have admitted I made a mistake and quit then. But I stayed, not wanting to give up on it, to be a quitter. When it was mutually agreed that I should leave, I left on a positive note. You may call my employer." Or, "I thought it was time for a change and I was looking around for a new job. It's common practice in that company that if they find out you are looking for another job, they ask you to leave." Should you claim a personality conflict? Most experts say *no*. Even if that *was* the reason you were fired, don't mention it. No one likes to think you are the kind of person who can't get along with others.

This question offers a good opportunity to mention to interviewers that they can call your former supervisor or employer. Ask your previous employers first, however. Let them know you are looking for another job and that you would appreciate their help in the form of a recommendation. If you don't want to give someone's name from a position where you were fired or didn't do well, don't. But remember that sometimes it's better to do so, especially if the interviewer knows you were fired. It's better that the interviewer *know* the worst than that he or she *imagine* the worst. The reality of the situation is always better than what he or she might imagine. And most former bosses are eager to be fair and honest on the job applicant's behalf, even in instances when there was a conflict.

Question 5. Is There Someone We Can Contact Who Is Familiar with You and Your Activities?

This question may be another way of finding out if you left your last job under good terms; so it is always helpful to cultivate and retain sympathetic allies at your last job. If the interviewer calls, the questions will center on your character, competence, stability, and special qualities relevant to the job. But, if you have had a number of jobs in the same field, feel free to give names from an earlier job too. Again, let them know they may be contacted.

Question 6. Where Do You See Yourself in the Company 10 Years from Now?

"In your chair" is the standard cute answer. However, not everyone will be amused. Think about what your real career plans are. Your answer should indicate that you are serious about working. Don't underestimate yourself. If this position is a step up on a specific corporate ladder, say so. The wrong answer might be that you want to remain in that same position, showing that you have no ambition. But, here again, there's no one right answer. Even if the job you're applying for involves a skill that doesn't apply to other jobs in the firm and is one that normally involves little mobility, in 10 years you could certainly expect to be training or supervising others doing that job.

Question 7. What Are Your Interests Outside of Work?

This is one of the more difficult questions to answer, even though it may sound deceptively simple. This question and its companion, "What do you do in your spare time?" are usually "fishing" questions. The interviewer cannot legitimately ask about your family, but if *you* bring it up, "Oh, I play tennis with my husband and son," then he or she can ask more questions. Keeping this in mind, you may decide not to mention your family at this time but to focus on your other interests and activities.

Your answers to this question can also backfire. Although the interviewer wants to think of you as someone who gets along with other people and has outside interests, it should not appear that you have *too many*. If you recite a long list of community involvements or leisure-time activities, the interviewer may well wonder when you will have time for work. When you practice this question, prepare to say something positive and specific about two or three activities you are involved in—particularly if you have been very successful at one of them.

Question 8. Why Do You Want to Work Here?

You will have to reconsider this question each time you go out on a different interview. As a general rule, do not say, "Because I need a job." (Remember, that's what Margaret said. If you are wondering what happened to Margaret, we sent her home, after her interview, to read this book and practice the techniques of job interviewing.) There is certainly nothing wrong with needing a job, but that is *not* what the interviewer wants to hear. Why would you like to work for this particular company? If you have done your research, you should know quite a lot about it and have an answer prepared. ("I think this would be a terrific place for me to use my accounting skills. I know that this division has recently expanded, and . . ." Or, "Some of my favorite books have been published by this company, and . . ." Or, "I really like what this company does for the community, and . . .") Remember, some subtle flattery may be in order here. The interviewer represents the company, and it will of course please him or her if you have something positive to say about it.

Question 9: Are You Applying to Other Companies?

If you are currently working and this is the only interview you have had, say so. They may be flattered. If you have had job offers, you can also share that. This question demands a simple, straightforward answer, and usually is not a problem for interviewee *or* interviewer.

Question 10. What Kind of Compensation Are You Looking For?

You know how to answer this question! (But if you haven't done your work on it yet, review the previous section and get started.)

Practice . . . Practice . . . Practice

The interviewer *can* ask hundreds of questions. No one asks them all, but you need to know the likeliest. To help you prepare, the following practice questions have been put in two categories.

The first list of forty-five questions is based on a Columbia University Graduate School of Business Survey in which a group of students were polled and asked about those questions thought to be the most difficult. In general, these questions are typical of ones you will be asked. You will recognize some of them from the first half of this chapter. (Some of these questions are also obviously based on a specific position; they are included to give you an even better sense of what can be asked.)

The second list gives thirty "stress interview" questions, which you are more likely to be asked when applying for a higher-level job, when it is assumed that you have had several jobs before. In this case, the interviewer may actually try to put you in a stressful situation. (Again, this practice is usually restricted to high-level positions.) The answer is not as important as *how* you respond. In *all* interview situations the interview is being used to predict your performance. In the case of the stress interview, the interviewer wants to see how you react—if you get rattled, stick firmly to your opinions, or are easily swayed.

Law school graduates, having passed school and bar exams, sometimes have to pass one more difficult test in order to land a good corporate job—the stress interview. The applicant is often grilled on a touchy subject during such an interview. One woman had to defend passage of the Equal Rights Amendment for about 20 minutes. She later found out that her interviewer is in favor of the ERA himself but was just trying to see how she reacted to stress! But don't worry, because stress interviews are currently out of style. And chances are that if you are faced with one, you'd cope very well with the added help of the advice in this book.

As you practice all these questions, remember that your manner, attitude, or "style" of answering is as important as *what* you actually say. If you respond with a brilliant answer but are hostile, the hostility is what will be heard. Don't worry about the exact wording of your replies, but be sure you have all the information you need to answer them. Think and respond positively (caution: the interview is not the place to air your negative feelings about your last job or your last boss). Your thoughtful attitude and willingness to answer well will impress your interviewer; so take your preparation seriously—it will help you to "pass" with flying colors.

Key Questions You May Be Asked in Interviews*

Personal Matters

1. Tell me about yourself. (Be prepared for this question and have your answer ready—for example, a short statement

*From the Columbia University Graduate School of Business.

saying where you were born, raised, and attended college, leading up to graduate school and why you are taking this interview. Please be imaginative.)

2. Describe your weaknesses. Describe your strengths. Your skills. (Try to show them to the best advantage in light of the company or industry you're talking to.)

3. What do you judge your major successes, accomplishments, to have been? Your failures? Your major disappointments?

4. What were the three most important events (decisions) of your life? What decisions have you most regretted? Why?

5. Are you a leader? Why do you say you are a leader? (Be prepared to give examples.)

6. What does your spouse do?

7. How did you like your summer (previous) job? What did you get out of it? What did you learn about yourself? What was the most rewarding thing about this (these) jobs? Why did you decide to leave it?

8. What makes you want to be a — (position applied for)?

9. How well do you work independently? With others?

10. If you could change the methods under which you work, what would you do?

11. How are you doing in your present job search?

12. What other organizations are you talking to?

13. What do you expect to get out of a career?

14. Where do you expect to be in 5, 10 years? On what do you base this?

15. You have five minutes to describe the most relevant and specific items in your background which show that you are uniquely qualified for this job.

16. Think of someone you dislike and tell me what makes you dislike this person so much.

17. Are you tough? Are you aggressive? (Be prepared to back up your answers.)

18. How competitive are you?

Education

19. Why did you choose — (your undergraduate college or university)?
20. Why did you major in art, history, etc.? With your background, why didn't you major in —?
21. If you were planning to go into business, why did you major in history, or — at the undergraduate level?
22. Do you think your grades are an indication of your academic achievement?
23. What courses have you taken in your major field? What electives?
24. What courses have you liked the most? The least?
25. Tell me about your high school years. Your college years.
26. What prompted you to get a degree in —?

Job—Company—Industry

27. Why are you interested in marketing? Why product management? Why advertising? Why finance? Why commercial banking? Why investment banking? Why corporate treasuryship? Why financial analysis? Etc.
28. Why are you interested in this industry? This particular company?
29. What do you think you will be doing in this job you are applying for? What do you think this job requires, and how do you match those requirements? What do you think the duties of someone who holds this job are? Why do you think you're suited for —?
30. How do you foresee the future of our industry?
31. How do you evaluate a business?
32. How do you judge a company when you are looking for a job?
33. Do you think a training program is useful? How do you evaluate a training program?

34. In addition to the company literature we sent out, to what sources did you go to find out about our corporation?
35. What have you read about our company, products, lately—outside of information in regular recruiting material?
36. In your research on our company, a. do you see any specific problems we have? b. is there any division in our organization that you are most interested in?
37. Do you think it was a good move for us to divest ourselves of the — division?
38. What are the differences between an account manager's job and a product manager's job? A commercial lender and an investment banker? A financial analyst and a securities analyst? A career in consulting versus a career with a corporation or a bank? Public accounting versus control? (Substitute pertinent jobs in your field.)
39. Why should we hire *you?*
40. Based on this interview, what questions do you have about the company?
41. What other questions do you have?

Location

42. Why do you want to stay in New York, relocate in Chicago, etc.?
43. Are you free to relocate? What constraints do you have?
44. How do you feel about job-related travel?
45. How does your family feel about your traveling?

Note: Again and again, both in the initial and the follow-up interviews, you must be able to answer effectively: Why this industry? Why this job? Why our firm?

Stress Interview Questions

1. What do you look for in a job?
2. Why are you leaving your present position?
3. What is your philosophy of management?
4. Do you prefer staff or line work? Why?
5. What kind of salary are you worth?
6. How long would it take you to make a contribution to our firm?
7. How long would you stay with us?
8. How do you feel about people from minority groups?
9. What new goals or objectives have you established recently?
10. How have you changed the nature of your job?
11. What do (did) you think of your boss?
12. Why haven't you obtained a job so far?
13. Would you describe a few situations in which your work was criticized?
14. How would you evaluate your present firm?
15. Do you generally speak to people before they speak to you?
16. What was the last book you read? movie you saw? sporting event you attended?
17. In your present position, what problems have you identified that had previously been overlooked?
18. Why aren't you earning more at your age?
19. Will you be out to take your boss's job?
20. Are you creative? (Give an example.)
21. Are you analytical? (Give an example.)
22. Are you a good manager? (Give an example.)
23. Have you helped increase sales? profits? How?
24. What do your subordinates think of you?
25. Have you fired people before?
26. Have you hired people before? What do you look for?
27. If you had your choice of jobs and companies, where would you go?

28. What other types of jobs are you considering? What companies?
29. Why do you feel you have top management potential?
30. What is more important to you, the money or the job?

Questioning Women

So far we have been dealing with the questions most people are asked at interviews. But as a woman you may be subjected to a whole barrage of questions never asked of a man.

Many have recounted horror stories of interview questions women have been subjected to in the very recent past. "Are you pregnant?" "Why do you want to take a job away from a man?" "Can we expect you to take off two days every month?" But the chances are now good that you will not be asked such blatantly discriminatory questions. However, it is true that you will be more closely questioned than a man about your ability to fulfill the requirements of your job and your family responsibilities.

Most of the worst forms of sex discrimination have been eliminated with the passage of laws and successful suits brought by women against their employers. But stereotypes die hard! Some of the problems you may face are based on a long tradition of what is thought to be appropriate for a woman. Research shows that many interviewers will judge the qualifications of a candidate against an implicit stereotype of what *they* consider to be the ideal candidate. For male Caucasian interviewers that ideal, not surprisingly, has often been "young," "white," and "male," particularly in traditional occupations. A survey confirming the existence of these biases was conducted in a university placement center. In that study recruiters were shown resumes of candidates with high, average, and low qualifications for a supervisory position. Women candidates were identical in qualifications to the men candidates, but the recruiters preferred the men. In a similar study, male college recruiters recommended hiring men over women for traditional male positions, but they were more likely to hire women as editorial assistants, traditionally a female position.

What about today? What can you expect? Over the past fifteen years business has been brisk at the government agencies charged with enforcing Equal Employment Opportunity (EEO) laws and regulations. Interestingly, it is the employment *selection* process that has been the target of many of the discrimination suits. (Industry is so vulnerable to charges of sex discrimination—although it is also subject to charges of age and race discrimination—that several pamphlets for interviewers have been prepared on how to avoid such suits. For example, "Conducting the Lawful Employment Interview: When Interviewing Job Candidates How to Avoid Charges of Discrimination," by Executive Enterprises Publications Co., Inc., 33 West 60 Street, New York, N.Y. 10023, 1974, and "Interviewing Women: Avoiding Charges of Discrimination," by Tom Jackson, also distributed by Executive Enterprises Publications, 1976.)

The Equal Employment Opportunity Legislation that affects us is Title VII of the Civil Rights Act of 1964, along with Executive Order 11246. Title VII applies to employers with more than fifteen employees and bans all discrimination in employment because of race, color, religion, *sex,* or national origin. It is administered by the Equal Employment Opportunity Commission. Executive Order 11246 covers employers with government contracts or subcontracts of more than $10,000 per year and similarly bans discrimination because of race, color, religion, sex, or national origin.

Before Title VII and Executive Order 11246, some employers tended to treat women as a *class,* not as individuals, and thus they could make generalizations about *all* women. One woman remembers being turned down in 1965 for a producer's job for a radio talk show host (who was noted, incidentally, for his "liberal" views). The reason? The host said, "We had a married woman here *once,* and she always had to go home early to cook for her husband. I'm really sorry you are married." Fortunately, that doesn't happen so much today, and if it did happen, the employer could be sued.

To understand the climate today, let's review the questions that are illegal (and some that are legal but may still be a problem for you) and how you should respond.

Illegal Questions

One problem in determining if a question is illegal is that federal laws are very general and subject to different interpretations. State laws are similarly vague and vary tremendously. Some states have individual Fair Employment laws that expressly forbid certain *types* of preemployment interview questions. However, there are questions that are illegal at job interviews but are perfectly legitimate *after* you are hired. For example, it may be necessary for the employer to know how many children you have and their ages for insurance purposes.

Under federal law there is *no* question that can *never* be asked. The usual test is: Does this question pertain to a "bona fide occupational qualification" (one that is mandatory for the job—for example, a women's room attendant must be a woman)?

Questions about the following areas are generally agreed to be considered discriminatory, or "suspect." Some questions are considered acceptable if they are asked of men as well as of women.* (If you are confused, you are in good company. This is a very tricky area.)

- Marital status questions, unless routinely asked of both men and women
- Contraception questions
- Reproductive questions: Are you planning to have children? More children? Etc.
- Child-care provision questions, unless also asked of men. The Supreme Court has ruled that an employer must *not*

---

*There are other categories of questions you *may not* be asked. A summary of the questions appears at the end of this chapter, reprinted from *California Women* have different hiring policies for men and women with preschool children.

To summarize: It is not just an individual question that is judged legal or illegal, but the implication and intent, and whether or not the question is asked of men as well. It *is* a tricky business.

Legal but Problematic Questions

The second group of questions are those which are legal but show prejudice and stereotypical attitudes. "Are you *really* sure you are available to travel?" is just one example. "Won't you be afraid to stay late?" is another. Remember that, as with any interview question, the underlying question actually being asked but not said out loud is: *"Are you as good a bet in which to invest time, training, and money?" And in this case the usual addition is "as a man would be?"*

Guidelines

If you keep the interviewer's underlying question in mind, you will have some guidelines as to how to answer. If you want the job, then you have to answer the question in a way that says, "Yes, I am a good bet." This would not be the occasion to fight for equal rights *unless* that is your goal. Ask yourself: What do I want to accomplish? If you definitely do not want the job, then you are free to make your response as strong as you wish.

Job Hint #4

As a job applicant, what can you do if you are asked an illegal question? The Wall Street Journal *pointed out you have three courses of action.*

1. Answer the question and ignore the fact that it is not legal.
2. Answer the question with the statement: I think that is not relevant to the requirements of the position.
3. Contact the nearest EEO Commission office.

Unless the violation is persistent, is demeaning, or you can prove it resulted in your not being employed, number three should probably be avoided. The whole area is too new; many interviewers are just not conversant with the code requirements. Answer number two is probably . . . the best to give. There are times when it may cost you the job, but are you interested in working for someone who is all that concerned about your personal life?"

—Richard Bolles, in
What Color is Your Parachute?
pp. 166–167

Another possibility to consider is that your interviewer is inept or amateur. Some interviewers told us they were just making "small talk" when they asked, "Are you married?" only to get the response: "Sir, do you know that is an illegal question?* I refuse to answer." Some questions, on the other hand, are not meant to pry into your personal life but are designed to tell the interviewer how much outside commitment you already have. One recruiter said, "If I ask about your family responsibilities, I just want to know how much time you will have for us. I wouldn't hire a single man who belonged to sixteen clubs. This is too demanding a business."

Remember, when you are being interviewed, you are also judging the company. If the interviewer insists on asking many "poor" questions, think: Do I really want to work for this

---

*It is not necessarily illegal unless asked only of women.

person? As one male recruiter put it, "Sure some organizations still discriminate. Try to discover that on the front end. Interview your interviewer. If he or she gets disturbed, doesn't that tell you something?"

Job Hint #5

(On the other hand . . .)
"Tell women not to come in with a chip on their shoulder. Some women are totally caught up in discussing the fact that they are women. They should never get hostile. They should consider whether the question is also addressed to men. I don't want to hire a woman who spends all of her energy talking about being a woman. I also wouldn't hire a man who talks and thinks about his masculinity all the time."

—Male Recruiter

Ten Questionable Questions

The following are ten questions you *may* be asked. Although you may hope that you never get any of them, practice your responses so that you will feel comfortable answering them. Your answers should show that: 1. you are ready and willing to work, and 2. you take yourself seriously. You may want to show that you consider some of the questions to be irrelevant and/or not work related, but only if you are very sure of yourself and the risk involved. How much risk you want to take will of course depend on how much you want or need the job.

1. What provisions have you made for your children?

LOW RISK: I have made arrangements for child care so that I can work.

effectively. That was one of the first things I took care of. I wouldn't be interviewing for a full-time position if I hadn't.

HIGH RISK: Do you also ask that question of men? I assure you I can handle this job.

2. What does your husband think of your going back to work?

LOW RISK: He approves and is very supportive, but I try to keep my home life and work life separate

HIGH RISK: I don't see how that question is relevant.

How would *you* answer these additional questions?

3. Are you willing to travel?
4. Are you planning more children? (Remember, this question is illegal, and so how do you want to respond?)
5. Tell me, are you married, single, divorced?
6. What would you do if your husband were transferred?
7. Why are you still single?
8. Our last girl always made coffee; you wouldn't mind, would you? (Note: It could actually be written into a job description that you make coffee. In that case it would be completely acceptable. The tricky part is if it is asked only of women.)

9. Do you receive alimony?
10. Our clients like to deal with men. Are you sure you can handle our customers as well as a man could?

Add any other similar questions you think you might be asked. And *practice*.

More conversation between Mr. Brown and Margaret . . .

Mr. Brown: Let's see, your resume doesn't include very much except your job with your uncle. What do you like to do in your spare time?
Margaret: Well, I take art courses and play tennis. Plus I spend a lot of time taking care of my house and my son Jimmy.
Mr. Brown: Oh, you have a son? How old is he?
Margaret: He was just six.
Mr. Brown: That's nice. They really are fun at that age. My kids are all grown up, now—but I liked it when they started school. Is he in school yet? I suppose you have someone take care of him?
Margaret: He just started school. I only recently decided to work full-time because I'm divorced and need the money. I haven't worked out all the arrangements with Jimmy yet.
Mr. Brown: Oh, you are divorced. How recently? I don't mean to pry but . . .

How would you rate this interview? Did Mr. Brown ask any illegal or poor questions? Was he just following up on Margaret's responses? What about Margaret? What do her answers indicate about her readiness to work?

Guide to Preemployment Inquiries

The May 1977 issue of *California Women* contained "Guidelines for Contemporary Employment Interviewing," based on a study conducted by the University of Wisconsin. Below is a "Guide to Preemployment Inquiries" taken from the State of California Fair Employment Practice Commission Rules and Regulations.

Acceptable Preemployment Inquiries	Subject	Unacceptable Preemployment Inquiries
"Have you worked for this company under a different name?" "Have you ever been convicted of a crime under another name?"	Name	Former name of applicant whose name has been changed by court order or otherwise.
Applicant's place of residence How long applicant has been a resident of this state/city	Address/ Duration of Residence	
"Can you, after employment, submit a birth certificate or other proof of U.S. citizenship or age?"	Birthplace	Birthplaces of applicant, applicant's parents, spouse, or other relatives Requirement that applicant submit a birth certificate, naturalization, or baptismal record prior to hire
"Can you, after employment, submit a work permit if under 18 years of age?" "Are you over 18 years of age?" "If hired, can you furnish proof of age?" or statement that hire is subject to verification that applicant's age meets legal requirements	Age	Questions which tend to identify applicants 40–64 years of age
	Religion	Applicant's religious denomination, church, pastor, parish, or religious holidays observed "Do you attend religious services/a house of worship?" Applicant may not be told "This is a Catholic/ Protestant/Jewish/atheist organization."

Lawful Inquiries	Subject	Unlawful Inquiries
Statement by employer of regular days, hours or shift to be worked	Work days and shifts	
"If you are not a U.S. citizen, have you the legal right to remain permanently in the U.S.? Do you intend to remain permanently in the U.S.?" Statement by employer that if hired, applicant may be required to submit proof of citizenship	Citizenship	"Are you a U.S. citizen?" Whether applicant, parents, or spouse are naturalized or native-born U.S. citizens Date when applicant or parents or spouse acquired citizenship Requirement that applicant produce naturalization papers or first papers Whether applicant's parents or spouse are citizens
	Race/Color	Complexion, color of skin, or other question directly or indirectly related to race or color
Statement that photograph may be required after employment	Photograph	Requirement that applicant affix a photograph to application form Request applicant, at her option, to submit photo Requirement of photograph after interview, but before hiring
Applicant's academic, vocational, or professional education; schools attended	Education	Date last attended high school

Acceptable Preemployment Inquiries	Subject	Unacceptable Preemployment Inquiries
Languages applicant speaks, writes, or reads fluently	National Origin/Ancestry	Applicant's nationality, lineage, ancestry, national origin, descent, or parentage Date of arrival in U.S./port of entry; how long a resident Nationality of applicant's parents or spouse; maiden name of applicant's spouse Language commonly used by applicant—"What is your mother tongue?" How applicant acquired ability to read, write, or speak a foreign language
Applicant's work experience Applicant's military experience	Experience	Type of military discharge
Names of applicant's relatives already employed by this company Name/address of parents or guardian if applicant is a minor	Relatives	Marital status or number of dependents Name/address of relatives, spouse, or children of adult applicant "With whom do you reside?" "Do you live with parents?"
"Have you ever been convicted of any crime?" "If so, when, where, and disposition of the case?"	Character	"Have you ever been arrested?"
Name/address of person to be notified in case of emergency	Notice in Case of Emergency	Name/address of relative to be notified in case of emergency

Organizations, clubs, professional societies or other associations of which applicant is a member, excluding any names the character of which indicate the race, religious creed, color, national origin, or ancestry of its members	Organizations	"List all organizations, clubs, societies and lodges to which you belong."
"By whom were you referred?"	References	Requirement of submission of a religious reference
"Do you have any physical condition which may limit your ability to perform job applied for?" Statement by employer that offer may be made contingent on passing a physical examination	Physical	"Do you have any physical disabilities?" Questions on general medical conditions Inquiries as to receipt of workmen's compensation
Notice to applicant that any misstatements or omissions of material facts may be cause for dismissal	Miscellaneous	Any inquiry that is not job related or necessary for determining an applicant's eligibility for employment

4 *THE FINAL STEPS*

Margaret is preparing herself for her second interview, enlisting the help of her friend Jan when necessary. She has not actively tried to schedule any further interviews until she rethinks her needs and defines her skills. Remembering her previous anxiety over the baby-sitter's arrival, Margaret has made arrangements to use an after-school child-care center in her neighborhood. (In fact, even though she doesn't have a job yet, Margaret has taken the chance of paying for the center's services now.) She has also rewritten her resume to include her volunteer experience and pertinent outside interests. To become more comfortable with the interview process, she practices answering questions, with Jan playing interviewer. Finally, Margaret answers an ad in the paper for a junior accountant at a chemical company. The interview is for the coming Friday. "What else must I do before then?" is her next question to herself.

Now that you have learned about the basic planning necessary for all interviews, it's time to learn preparation techniques for each specific interview. In contacting potential employers, you have a simple goal: to set up job interviews. You should request interviews from all employers who have received your resume, and follow up this way on job leads—no matter what the source.

Some companies may contact you first, but be prepared to telephone them yourself. Set aside a block of time expressly for making calls and receiving return calls. You may want to schedule times for return calls (remaining flexible of course to employers' schedules): "Would you please have Mr. Smith call me back between two and three this afternoon?" (Do not leave messages for them to return your call and then tie up the phone with other calls. If an employer has many job candidates to contact and your wire is busy, he or she may not call you back.) Treat each call as the first stage of your interview, since it is your first verbal contact with the employer and therefore a test of your telephone communication skills. Several interviewers told us they could tell from a brief telephone conversation that someone was going to be terrific.

A good "telephone communicator" has the ability to express herself clearly and concisely in a voice that is at once relaxed and energetic (neither so slow that you deliberate over every word, nor so fast that you give the impression that you have to board a train within minutes of the conversation). Your telephone voice should reflect confidence and certainty, and perhaps cheerfulness. To practice these traits, use a cassette player to record yourself. Change your words and your voice level, adding or decreasing the degree of expressiveness. You might also follow Margaret's example and ask a friend to listen to you. If after your "rehearsals" you still find that you have "stage fright," don't hesitate to write a script for what you want to say and follow it until you feel comfortable.

The idea is to know whom you want to reach and to start by explaining your purpose: "Hello, my name is Margaret Peters. I'm responding to the ad for a junior accountant in the Sunday *Times*. It sounded very interesting and appropriate for me. I'd like to come in for an interview." Or, "Hello, this is Margaret Peters. I sent a letter and resume to you last week at the suggestion of Jan Smith. I would like to set up an appointment for an interview."

Realize that *your* goal and *the employer's* goal may be quite different. You want an appointment, so you are hoping not to spend too much time answering or asking questions at this time. The employer, however, may want to use the telephone to screen out as many candidates as possible. In case you do have to elaborate, therefore, know as much as you can about the employing organization and the job requirements. Your degree of information will depend largely on how you heard about the job. If your contact is through an employment agency or a knowledgeable friend, you may be well informed; if you are calling in response to a newspaper ad, you may not even know the name of the firm. In any event, be prepared to answer the basic "Tell me about yourself" (in abbreviated form)—including your experience and background. (Remember, employers are rightly not interested in the candidate who lacks appropriate qualifications.)

When scheduling your appointments, make sure you know the "facts" before you hang up: who, where, when, what time. (Use the forms in Chapter 5 for recording this information.)

Next, complete your research in these three areas:

1. *Before being interviewed you should know WHO will interview you.* The first person you meet may be a representative of the personnel department, well trained in the art of interviewing (that is what he or she does for a living). In that case, you will be "screened" and, we hope, introduced to someone more directly related to your position. If the personnel department is your first stop, you are likely to have a structured interview. At the very least, the interviewer will have many questions ready. Although this person may or may not know the specifics of a job, he or she will certainly know all about the company. So be attentive! You can learn much of what you will need to know at this interview.

The higher the position, the more likely that your first interview will be with your future boss.* Often these interviews are unstructured; some executives really are not good at interviewing, do not like to hire people, and could therefore be under great stress.

Still another possibility is that you will be interviewed jointly by several people. Chapter 5 covers this special situation.

---

*Companies vary, but at very high levels, you may have to survive two or three different interviews.

Whatever the circumstances may be, it is important to know them beforehand.

2. *You must know as much as possible about the NATURE OF THE JOB.* One good way to do this is simply to ask if you may see a job description before the interview. For most corporate jobs it will include the job requirements and responsibilities. Familiarize yourself with whatever material is available so that you understand both the skills needed and the "jargon" of the field. For example, publishing has a whole "alphabet" of proofreading terms, whereas computer people are always talking about such things as "hardware" and "software." Write down any questions you may have about the job on an index card and ask for clarification during the interview. One of your first questions could be: "This is what I have been told [or: This is what I understand . . .] about the position; is that the way *you* see the job?"

3. *You must know as much as possible about the COMPANY OR ORGANIZATION.* From your preliminary research, stressed in Chapter 2, you should be familiar with a company to which you apply. An excellent way to find out about an organization is simply to ask for information when you schedule the appointment. If the person with whom you talk is too busy, ask to speak to the secretary. Explain to her that you have an interview and would like whatever company information is readily available—brochures, annual reports, etc. Ask politely but forthrightly. You have no "ulterior motives" to conceal.

One interviewer, in fact, tells us she hired the librarian who had researched the company beforehand in its own library. Another candidate for business manager impressed the hiring committee with her typed list of specific questions on the company's financial position. (This also showed *her* understanding of the position of business manager.)

Job Hint #6

"I was counseling a woman the other day and I realized I knew more about her 'specialty' than she did. I asked, 'Why aren't you keeping up with the literature, and going to conferences?' Job hunters need to know something about the current 'state of the art' of their field."
— Sharon Bermon
Counseling Women

Finally, don't mistakenly assume that *all* jobs in one category are so similar that it is not necessary to do your homework. For example, if you are interviewing for a teaching position, carefully research every school and its community (this research will also help you choose between one position and another).

These questions will help you plan your research:

1. How large is the organization?
2. How long has it been in business?
3. What is the reputation of the company?
4. What are its products/services?
5. What is the management like?
6. Does it have regional or branch locations?

Add additional questions specific to each interview as you do your preliminary research.

Based on your preparation, jot down on an index card a brief list of questions about the company to bring with you to the interview. Remember, even though your skills and needs stay the same, you must do research for each interview.

As a final check of your interest in the position and your readiness for each interview, fill out the Position Form found on page 157. It will help you answer the crucial deciding questions: Do you want this job? Are you qualified for the job? Are you suited to this company?

Role Playing

An excellent way to become aware of how an interviewer might see you and to give yourself a final rehearsal before the interview is to role play. And by playing both the interviewer and the interviewee, you can gain special, dual insight into the interview process. Chances are good that you know at least one other person who is looking for a job. Pair up with a friend or friends, have some fun role playing, and share your experiences for the feedback needed to improve.

Begin by exchanging resumes and taking turns interviewing each other. Select one of our sample jobs or one that you clip from a newspaper want ad. Conduct a brief interview using the questions in Chapter 3—and make up some of your own. You may want to tape record the sessions so that you can hear how others hear you. Remember, the skill of verbal communication (ease and articulateness in talking) is used by many interviewers as one measure of intelligence.

Listen to the tape. How do you sound? Is your voice level (pitch) too low or too high? Are you speaking too fast? Pausing too much ("As I, uh, was, uh, saying, uh . . .")? Or are you pleased with your poise and presence? The more you practice, the better you will sound.

Ask yourself what you have learned, not only about yourself, but also as interviewer. What would you look for in a job candidate that you can apply to your interview performance? (Even if you do not have someone to practice with, it is still important to do this role playing for interviews. Sit down with a tape recorder and ask yourself questions.)

We have included scenarios for two role plays here to stimulate your imagination and boost your "interview I.Q." (Actors often attend "How to Audition" classes where the students rate each other on the basis of readings and interviews and then discuss whether the auditioner would have been "called back" and/or hired for a part.) Although you may not know the specifics of the occupations, you will be able to think of the right types of questions and answers. Remember to take turns being the interviewer and the applicant. As the interviewer, ask yourself what skills the person should have for the job, what impresses you, what you are looking for. When you are through, give each other feedback. Would you have hired your friend and would he or she have hired you? Why?

Use a form like this one for each position you interview for. Make a page in your notebook and fill it in like this as an aid for the interview and as a record for yourself. You could also copy these pages to insert in your notebook.

Position Form

Position _____

Industry _____

A. <u>The Technical Qualifications</u> (What are the minimum requirements for you to fulfill this job? Do you need a degree? Special training?) _____

_____

_____

B. <u>Working Conditions</u> (What can you expect at this job? What are the normal hours, surroundings, etc.?) _____

_____

_____

C. <u>Knockout Factors</u> (List those qualities which would make you clearly ineligible for this position. For example, fear of flying for a stewardess.) _____

_____

_____

D. <u>Compensation</u> (What can you expect in terms of salary range and fringes? Some industries have "special" benefits. For example, universities give free tuition. What is *your* acceptable salary for this position?) _____

_____

_____

E. Career/Promotion Possibilities (What is the next position above this one likely to be?
Where could you go from here?) _____

_____

_____

F. Are you still interested in this job? Are you qualified for it? _____

_____

_____

Role Play # 1

Spend a few minutes reviewing these roles and then conduct a
15-minute interview; one person takes the role of employer and
another the role of applicant.

**The
Employer**   Your company, the Prince Corporation, is an "old
line" conservative manufacturer of lighting fixtures
and systems for industrial establishments. Customers range in size from corporations of 75–100
employees to major corporations with multiplant
installations.

Sixty-five percent of your sales are to architects,
engineers, and builders connected with original
plant construction, and the balance is in updating
existing lighting in older plants.

At present your sales are concentrated mainly in the
Midwest but, in line with corporate objectives, have
been expanding into the rest of the nation. Corpo-

rate sales have risen to $75 million from $60 million two years ago.

The Position

Assistant Sales Manager. This position calls for a person with a technical background who has had direct sales experience with the type of customers you now have and hope to obtain as part of your growth. The field sales force now includes ten salespersons (all men) who work on their own but must be kept motivated and informed. The Assistant Sales Manager will be responsible for direct liaison with the sales force, for recruiting new field sales staff, and for implementing sales programs which have been approved by the Sales Manager.

The person employed will travel approximately eight to ten days per month and will also be responsible for the training and motivation of both new and old salespersons.

The salary is $15,000 per year plus an incentive bonus based on increased sales. This bonus could add as much as an additional $8,000 per year to the salary.

The Applicant

You have answered a newspaper advertisement and have been invited in on the basis of the following brief resume.

MAXINE COLLIER

Education: BS, Lehigh University, 1967, Architecture

Experience: Not presently employed.

October 1972–1975: Sales Manager, Architectural Products, Inc.

Supervised a sales force of five persons involved in selling lighting fixtures to large housing developments and schools. Personally recruited, hired, and trained new salespersons. Sales volume increased during my tenure from $8 million to $12 million, including two government contracts which represented new business for the corporation.

1970–1972: Designer, Pratt and Pratt, an architectural firm

Responsible for engineering, estimation, systems design, proposal preparation, and overseeing the installation of heating and ventilating systems.

1968–1969: Layout Artist, Biegler, Brown, and Rogers

Did layouts and renderings for this small architectural firm.

Role Play #2

The Employer

The Stillwell Hospital Center is a 350-bed hospital which will be completed within six months. It is part of a larger medical organization affiliated with a major university. Although for the first few months the new hospital will be under the administrative control of the university, the plan is for the hospital to be completely independent of day-to-day control within one year of opening.

The hospital will be one of the most modern facilities of its kind with the strongest possible financial foundation. In terms of administrative management, the objective is to use the most sophisticated management techniques; computerized personnel and accounting records; and an advance pharmaceutical purchase, inventory, and control system.

You are working temporarily as Personnel Manager for the hospital. You work for the Acting Director.

The Position

Business Office Manager. Responsible for patient admissions, patient and third-party billings, credit and collections, cash forecasting, and related systems and procedures, including the hiring of administrative staff. Must have college degree with study in related field. Four to six years' experience in hospital administration is essential. Knowledge of computer systems is desired.

Position offers an excellent opportunity to apply new ideas in a progressive environment.

Salary between $14,000 and $20,000 plus good fringe benefits and free medical care.

NOTE: Stillwell Hospital has been built over the objections of conservation groups who did not want their park torn down and are objecting to the increased noise. The applicant may have to pass through a demonstration.

The Applicant

RAMONA RODRIGEZ, MAJOR

Career Objective	To translate over twelve years of health-care experience into productive work with an organization in the health-care field.
Education	University of Pennsylvania, 1961, BA Public Health Temple University, 1963, MA Management Medical Services Administrative Training Program 1966–67 (Special program for staff-level Army Medical Officers conducted in cooperation with the Walter Reed Medical Center).
Experience	1965–1977: Women's Army Corps Current Rank: Major 1972–1977: Administrative Officer, Amarillo Base Hospital Set up and administered all aspects of hospital management, including all record-keeping procedures in accordance with hospital operating manual and specifications.

Designed new system to handle processing of large number of Vietnam veterans who were processed out of this base in 1972–73.

Served as consultant to base commander on health and recreation policy.

1965–1972: Assistant Officer in Charge, Personnel Records Division, U.S. Army Command Center, Washington, D.C.

Was responsible for implementing the transition from a manual personnel records system to a computer and microfilm system designed by the Control Data Corporation.

Salary   Negotiable.

Dressing for the Part

Looking "good" will not automatically guarantee you employment, but looking "bad" often results in an immediate negative decision. And your wardrobe *is* one area over which you have total control. Unfortunately, there is no magic outfit designed for instant job hiring, but beware! There are clothes that will act to eliminate you for some positions. As Tom Jackson says, "The way you present yourself is the single most powerful nonverbal statement you make about yourself."

Every interviewer had stories to tell of inappropriately dressed applicants. "She came dressed in a T-shirt and jeans. Although she was actually more qualified than the woman we hired, her appearance projected: 'I don't really care about this job; I don't take this, or myself, very seriously!'" Thus, if you *insist* on wearing jeans, don't be surprised if the company insists on hiring someone else. Studies report that interviewers react negatively to jeans and extremely casual clothes.

Several experts recommend that you figure out how you would dress if you were already working at the company and then dress just a little better. (As Sharon Bermon says, "Dress as if you *already* had the *next* position.") In addition, although dress codes do vary, almost every industry has a "uniform." At one point, people joked about the IBM uniform—white button-down shirt, conservative two-piece suit, etc. In contrast, an advertising agency's "with-it" look might be much less regulated. (As part of your research, also try to find out what the organization's "uniform" looks like.)

In general, however, the rule of thumb is: Dress conservatively. Wear subdued, solid colors and well-tailored clothes, preferably a suit or dress with matching jacket. A popular "how-to-dress" book advocates a strict adherence to an interview "uniform" that depends on the industry, time of year, and locale. The author insists you leave nothing to chance and details how each item of clothing "tests" with employers.

Experts do disagree at times. One recruiter advises you to "dress so that the interviewer doesn't remember what you wore," while another believes that at times you *should* dress to stand out (favorably, of course), particularly when competing with many applicants. One organization hired the one woman among twenty applicants they remembered best—the only one *not* wearing jeans. Later they learned that she had wisely borrowed a suit for the occasion.

In selecting clothes, one of the most important rules is to feel comfortable. If a particular dress or skirt is going to make you miserable, causing you to spend half your time pulling and tugging at it, wear something else! Furthermore, it is a good idea not to surprise yourself by going to an interview wearing something for the first time, not even a new brand of stockings that may turn out to be too baggy or snug. Break in those shoes the day before so you are free from pinched toes (or nerves) the day of the interview.

As part of a total picture, your clothes should reflect a confident but not blasé attitude. "I can take this job or leave it" is an impression you want to *avoid*. Being hired for a good position that interests you is important, and you should dress well for the occasion. On the other hand, save your party clothes for a party. One interviewer commented, "She looked really beautiful, but I thought she had mistaken our office for a discotheque." You mean business, and that's the message your clothes should project. To that end, you might want to carry a briefcase, even if it contains only a few extra copies of your resume and your notes. The interview is an investment in your future. It might well be worth one or two outfits bought especially for job interviews.

Job Hint #7

"Do not sabotage yourself. Most people dress generally at the level at which they are stuck. Dress the way you would if you succeeded in obtaining all the things you wanted to obtain in the next two years. If you dress that way now—you'll look like you've already gotten there."
—Tom Jackson

And listen to your interviewers, particularly if your first contact is with personnel people, who know what the appropriate dress is. If they suggest you wear something else, don't get defensive; change clothes. They're interested! One personnel manager recounted: "One candidate who was especially suitable for the position had on sunglasses and espadrilles. She actually looked all right, but this company is a very formal one where people dress up. So she would have a better chance, I asked her to come back for another appointment."

A parting thought on this topic comes from Tom Jackson: "I can walk into a company and meet eight people. I can tell by the way they dress and handle their bodies* who among them are going to be a success."

*For some advice on body language, see the next chapter.

How Would You Handle These Situations?

Jane has been working part-time for an importer for several years. Recently, she has been looking for full-time employment with more responsibility. Although she usually wears a skirt and blouse or dress to work, since today is inventory day, she is wearing a casual sweater and slacks. While she is counting boxes, an employment agency calls to send her for a job interview at 3 that afternoon. Anxious, Jane goes out at lunchtime and buys a new shirt. She still doesn't feel comfortable. At the interview, she begins by explaining why she is wearing slacks. The recruiter is impressed by her forthright handling of a potentially awkward situation; he hires her on the spot.

Jane could have postponed the interview for another day, bought a dress, or simply gone as she was. Her "compromise" worked well for her.

What would you have done?

Rita K. faces a similar situation. An employment agency has a perfect job possibility for her. Considering what she is wearing too casual for the blue-chip firm that has the job opening, her agency counselor suggests that she go home and change to a suit before reporting to the interview. Dismayed, Rita confesses she doesn't have a suit. The solution: Generously, the counselor offers to lend her an appropriate outfit for the day. Rita gets the job. (She will spend the next day shopping for some well-tailored clothes.)

Preparation is the key to successful interviewing, whether you're researching a company or deciding what to wear. The next chapter will give you some final hints on last-minute preparation and on the actual interview itself.

5 THE DAY OF THE INTERVIEW

Margaret is ready. Prior to the interview she found out who her interviewer will be, and for several days has rehearsed question after question. With plenty of time and good directions, she arrives early enough to park her car at a one-hour meter, stop for a cup of coffee, and then freshen up in the women's room. Proceeding to the company's offices, she greets the receptionist with a smile and meets her interviewer, Ms. Green, the chemical company's business manager. (Margaret has one uncomfortable moment when she is unexpectedly asked to take a bookkeeping-accountant test. However, she finds the questions relatively easy and routine.) This time, when asked to "tell me about your accomplishments," Margaret answers easily. Ms. Green introduces her to other staff members and suggests a tour of the plant. Margaret decides to risk a parking ticket (her meter time is up) and agrees. At the end of the interview, Margaret asks when their decision will be made. Ms. Green says, "I can let you know early next week. Please call me." They shake hands warmly. Margaret is pleased; whether or not she is hired for this job, she knows she did well at the interview.

Your day has arrived. Obviously, you should be on time, and what that really means is about 15 minutes early. Even with the best excuse in the world, being late gets the interview off to a poor start. Also, make sure you schedule enough time in your day for the interview itself. Allow an *extra* hour for contingencies: The interviewer may be delayed or may want to give you a tour or introduce you to other people. Especially if you are doing well, you don't want to have to leave and then come back, unless specifically asked to do so.

What to Bring with You

Before you leave for the interview, make certain you have everything you will possibly need.

1. *Pens and notepad:* Taking notes for the greater part of your interview can be distracting, rude, and plain silly. *Don't.* However, if there is a specific point or two to remember or follow up, do jot it down.
2. *Extra copies of your resume:* Don't assume that the interviewer still has your resume available. Always bring more.
3. *Index cards:* You should bring a. a card with the 4 or 5 points about yourself you want to cover; b. a card with your questions about the position; c. a card with 4 to 5 questions about the company that demonstrate your preplanning; d. a card with all the necessary data for any application forms you might have to complete, including your Social Security number, the date and place of your birth, dates and addresses of schools you attended, and years of graduation.
4. *Supporting material:* This additional material may be in the form of a portfolio or may take many forms: a report you compiled, an article you wrote, a sample of your work—any concrete examples you have of your achievements and talents. Although you may not need these samples, it's a good idea to bring them along. It's very impressive to the interviewer when you can offer such visible proof of your abilities, even if all you are showing is that you have worked on various things (they can be as routine as typing or writing different kinds of letters) and are prepared to show them.
5. *The names and addresses of your references:* Have a typed list of references available to leave at the end of the interview. Depending on the interview and your resources, you may want to have a few different lists to substitute. Usually, three or four "good" references suf-

fice. Choose your references wisely; a good reference is someone who knows you personally, can discuss your work, and has agreed to be a reference. (Be sure you notify everyone you plan to use. One woman lost her chance for a job because her "celebrity" reference could hardly remember her when called by the interviewer.) Do not list friends for whom you then claim you've worked as references. You will almost certainly be caught. (But do use friends as personal references if required.)

Note: With regard to your personal and professional data: the higher the position, the more likely that all details about you will be checked. In any case, it is not unusual for the employer to verify your academic degrees. (And one newly hired woman we spoke to was asked to bring her masters degree and birth certificate the first day she started work.)

The Interview—The Beginning

When you arrive, cordially greet the receptionist, secretary, or whoever is there to receive you. Be polite and friendly to everyone. Not only will you work with these people if you do get the job, but also they may be asked for their opinions of you. Your nervousness might be perceived as "snobbishness" by an unwitting secretary. It could cost you the job. So begin the interview in effect when you walk in the door.

Actually, the first phase of the interview itself begins before any questions are even asked. You are being judged from the initial contact, and these impressions have a significant influence (remember those famous first four minutes). Now is the time to establish rapport. Start with a *firm* handshake (jobs really have been won or lost on the basis of handshakes). Your opening conversation in the office can involve small talk—about the current snowstorm, a championship game, the Oscars, etc. Have a few openers handy, and use them if needed. If you are offered your choice of seats, take the one closest to the interviewer's desk. If your chair is in an uncomfortable place—directly in the sun, for example—ask to move it. Do not smoke unless the interviewer is smoking. Do not even ask if you may smoke if the interviewer isn't smoking. (Smoking is offensive to many people regardless how polite they are about it. Also you may find yourself awkwardly searching for an ashtray.)

Transition to the second stage, or the body, of the interview can sometimes be awkward. If the small talk continues too long, it's a good idea to open a more serious discussion by saying, "Shall I begin to tell you about myself?"

Job Hint #8

"If you are nervous, it is all right to say so. The interviewer probably knows it anyway, and it may just be making him or her more nervous too!"

—Tom Jackson

The Body of the Interview

At this stage, the majority of questions are asked and answered by both sides. Within 15 minutes the quality of your answers should convey the impression: "I am the woman who can do this job. I would be an asset to the company." Avoid giving the message either that you are interested only in what the company can do for you or that the company has more to offer than you have to give.

1. Within the context of a dialogue, you and the interviewer are both asking questions. Listening well is a necessary skill here. If you don't understand a point, ask for clarification. Be frank. If you are really thrown a curve, it is perfectly acceptable to say, "I have never considered

that before." In fact, consider your answers carefully and when necessary answer in depth. However, monitor yourself. Although you want to cover the various aspects of a question, don't overanswer. Interviewers recalled candidates who talked endlessly when a simple yes or no would have been sufficient. In turn, pose relevant, necessary questions. The answers to your questions should furnish you with information to help you sell yourself; so be attentive. And remember, throughout this phase you are also engaged in conversation. You can pause and reflect a moment, ask another question, or even make a joke.

2. Be sure you understand the nature of the position. If you did not find out beforehand, simply ask: "Could you tell me what this job entails and the kind of skills you're looking for?" Listen carefully to the answer; then describe your skills and experience in the employer's terms, using the interviewer's vocabulary when appropriate. The interviewer can give you the clues to the "right" answers.

3. Make sure you understand the career possibilities. As Linda Kline remarked, "Women think it is very aggressive to ask about promotional opportunities or to find out, for example, why this job is available or what happened to the last person who had it. If you are told that the last 18 people previously holding the job were fired, you'll know something more about the stress level of the work environment. If the previous person was promoted, you'll know there is the possibility of mobility."

4. If the interviewer or interviewers have not asked you the question, "Tell me about yourself," then ask "Would you like me to tell you about myself?" Impress them, whenever possible, with the depth and range of your experience and accomplishments. Remember the advice from Chapter 3, and be specific. There is no need to recite your resume. Some sample statements: "I handled all the publicity for the national trade show. We had over 250 exhibits and had coverage in five papers including *The New York Times.*" Or, "In the year I held that position, I

raised more than $300,000." Or, "During the time I was sales manager, sales went up nearly 40 percent." Prepare these answers ahead of time to fit your experiences. Note, too, that businesspeople relate to numbers, so remember to quantify your accomplishments. Use this opportunity to tell them why you want to work for the company and what you can do for them.

5. Make sure you can explain any gaps in your resume. Bring up any "problem areas" before the interviewer asks you about them. "You are probably wondering about that one-year gap in my resume. I was traveling and . . ."

6. Make sure you have all the information you need before you leave. Do not leave the interview without knowing:

The company's general environment
Your responsibilities
Promotion possibilities
Training
The job potential
Your authority
Job requirements
Travel expectations

The Final Phase

The final phase of the interview begins with the windup questions during the interview and doesn't end until a decision has been reached after the interview. Many people do not know how to handle this last stage of the interview well. Experts told us that often candidates will "foreclose" the interview too soon. As it becomes clear that you are winding up, ask for feedback or an assessment of your chances. Tom Jackson reminds us: "It is O.K. to ask, toward the end of the interview, 'Do you think I have the qualifications you are looking for?'" You may even be able to correct instantly a wrong impression. For example, "Yes I *do* have experience in speaking before groups. I should have mentioned that I was on the debating team at college."

In addition, do not shortchange yourself. Get all the information you need before you leave, so that if they offer you a position, you'll have enough information on which to base a decision. One woman surprised her interviewer by asking to meet the people she would be supervising if she got the job. (They thought it was a good idea and agreed.) And, if you are really interested in the job, *ASK FOR IT!* Let the interviewer know that you want it and that you are confident enough to ask.

Find out what your next steps should be and who should initiate them. Is the interviewer expecting you to mail him/her something (e.g., design samples, publicity releases, charts)? How soon? If you are expecting another job offer soon, and you would prefer this one, tell the interviewer. It may hasten a decision on your behalf.

A Word about Nonverbal Communication

So far we have been dealing with verbal communications, but many important messages are also conveyed in a nonverbal manner. Remember the old cliches "Actions speak louder than words" and "A picture is worth a thousand words"? What are you saying with your body?

Results of recent tests show that high-verbal interviewees score much higher with interviewers than low-verbal candidates and are much more likely to be considered for a job. High-*non*-verbal behavior is also a deciding factor in favorably rating candidates. Good eye contact, varied voice modulation, high energy level expressed through (modified) gestures, smiling, and other active responses are rated high. Low-nonverbal inter-viewees demonstrate little energy or interest; they avoid eye contact and speak hesitantly. No one who participated in one test would have invited back the low-nonverbal candidates.

Various books now on the market purport to "interpret" every conceivable gesture or "body language," and although the idea may seem strange at first, you can learn to talk with your body. A general knowledge of body language "vocabulary" is a useful aid in analyzing both your behavior and another person's. Review some common nonverbal communications and what they communicate.

1. *Posture.* Your posture is a very noticeable part of you and "speaks" immediately about your attitude toward yourself and your situation. Sitting up straight and erect conveys a professional, businesslike attitude, while slouching signifies lack of attention, indifference, and possibly a sense of intimidation.

2. *Eyes.* We speak with our eyes. The eyes are the most important part of the body for establishing direct rapport. Look your interviewer in the eye. Make sure, however, you don't start a staring contest. (One writer suggests looking at your interviewer's nose instead. It will look as if you are looking into his/her eyes.)

3. *Hands.* Some people are naturally more animated than others and use their hands to be expressive. Again, be yourself, but if you are prone to using your hands excessively, keep them in your lap. Do not be caught flailing around and gesturing wildly. Also be wary of touching your interviewer (or being touched). Touching (other than your firm handshake) will be interpreted as inappropriately intimate behavior for an interview.

Other hints: Smiling is usually contagious. It communicates confidence in yourself. So smile. It's much harder to dislike or ignore a smiling person. And practice your firm sincere handshake with friends and family (shake hands with both men and women).

Interviewers communicate nonverbally also, and you can pick up messages from them. Some positive signs are smiling and eye contact from the interviewer. Among the negative clues are nervous gestures like tapping on the table, folded arms, clock watching—and, of course, yawning! If your interviewer is distracted or bored, you will have to regain his/her attention. In that case try asking a pertinent question, saying, "Would you like to hear more about my experience?" or even simply raising your own voice level a bit and exhibiting more energy yourself. If you are energetic, the interviewer is more likely to be energetic as well.

Special Situations

At some point in the interview you may be asked to take a test. This procedure is often routine, and sometimes the outcome is completely irrelevant. (One woman who was concerned at having to take a personality test was once told, "Don't worry, no one has ever looked at the results.") Aptitude tests are occasionally administered before you meet the interviewer. Civil Service exams are of course a required part of the hiring process for government jobs.

When setting up the interview, ask if you are expected to take a test, and if so inquire about the nature of the test. If during the course of an interview the test comes as a complete surprise, you may ask if you can come back and take it later, particularly if the test requires extensive preparation on your part. Secretaries are usually asked to take typing tests, and other types of skills are routinely tested.

When applying for an editorial position or one requiring writing, you might be given "homework." Consider this a good sign. Make sure you understand exactly *what* is expected and *when* the assignment should be returned. One woman never asked when her writing assignment was due and found out someone else had been hired while she was still completing her work. (If you are asked to do anything excessive—for example, to edit an entire manuscript or run an errand—be honest and stand up for yourself. Start off on the right foot and the chances are you will not be taken advantage of if you do get the job.)

Lunch Interviews

At high job levels you might be invited to lunch as a first or last step in the interview process. There you may find yourself being observed by several people. Lunch interviews are routine if you will be expected to take clients out as part of your job. Again, remember that the interview is used as a measure to predict your performance. Take your cue from the interviewer about whether or not to order a drink before lunch. One recruiter advises his clients to order if the interviewer does, ask for the same drink as the interviewer, and then to "pour it in a plant" when no one is looking. No one wants to be impaired by a drink at such an important time as an interview. And obviously if you are not comfortable drinking and don't want to pretend, order a soft drink or mineral water, without defensiveness or excuses. If you are not sure what entree to order, again take your cue from the people around you by simply letting them order first. You don't want to be the one waiting for a well-done steak while they all eat salads. (Courtesy may force them to let their soup grow cold while they wait for you to be served!) Since it is a tricky feat to talk and eat at the same time, pick something easy to handle and take small breaks between bites to answer or ask a question.

Job Hint #9

"Never order anything that drips, takes too much time to prepare, or is messy."

—Linda Kline
Maximus Consulting, Inc.

Group Interviews

Group or panel interviews in which you meet two or more people are usually more expensive for the employer and difficult to arrange, so they are not conducted routinely. They are, however, used fairly often in the academic world, some social service organizations, and certain other organizations. The system is considered by some to be a fairer method of evaluation. In a group interview you have a chance to relate to and impress more than one person, and the responsibility of hiring rests with several people. Also, in group interviews you may receive a clearer picture of the composition and style of the organization so you can more easily know whether it's what you are looking for.

Under the best circumstances you will know whether you will face an individual or a group of people before your appointment. Ask at your first contact: "Would you mind telling me how I will be interviewed, by one or by several people? I'd like to be as prepared as possible." If you are a naturally extroverted person, you might enjoy the panel experience more and do particularly well.

Most of the same rules apply for group interviews as for single-interviewer situations. A group interview may seem more intimidating, but if you do succeed and look good, you will look doubly or triply good. After you are introduced, write down everyone's name in your notepad in their seating order. Don't rush; take your time answering the questions even though you may be asked more of them. Again, pay attention to the "body language" you are projecting. Don't slouch; remember: It can indicate that you are intimidated. Maintain eye contact with each person as he/she talks to you. Watch your focus: Even if you sense the approval of one person, do not take that as a cue to direct all your remarks to her/him. Listening well is especially important, so that you can make comments such as: "Mr. Green, you should be interested in my accounting skills, since you asked that question earlier about . . ." Think of the group interview as an informal conference where you are one of the panelists (instead of a den of wolves with you as the lone lamb). Actually, the main difference between the group and the individual interview is that you'll have more hands to shake and more eyes to contact, so keep smiling.

After Each Interview: Interview Feedback and Follow-Up

Margaret goes home and shares her experience with her trusted friend Jan.

Margaret: "Well, I guess I'll just have to wait until next week."

Jan: "Don't forget to drop a note to Ms. Green."

Margaret: "Why?"

Jan: "Do you want the job, Margaret?"

Margaret: "Yes; of course."

Jan: "O.K., then, ask for it."

The interview may be over, but your work isn't. First, give yourself interview feedback. Remember the advice from Chapter 1: No one expects you to land your first job at your first interview. What you *are* expected to do is to use each interview as a learning experience, meeting new people and learning about various industries and positions.

Fill out your Interview Rating Form page 183 and Interview Record Form page 181. Your Rating Form is a personal exercise designed to help you. No one else will ever see it. If you "fluffed" this interview, it is okay. But profit from your mistakes by analyzing where you went wrong. The form will help you see your mistakes more clearly.

Second, you must do interview follow-up! Note any necessary follow-up on the Interview Record Form. If you have been asked to call or send materials or to return anything, do so promptly. You must continue to make a good impression even if you have not actually been granted the job. A sympathetic or interested interviewer may recommend you for another position.

We hope that sending a brief note after each interview has

become an increasingly "routine" practice for you. The note may serve a two-fold purpose, extending a basic courtesy to your interviewer and giving you an opportunity to correct an erroneous impression by adding information. For example, "When I looked over the materials you gave me, I noticed that the company has periodic public fund-raising drives. I thought you might be interested in my fund-raising experience. As Chair of the fund-raising committee for the PTA, I helped raise over $20,000. . . ." Or "I hope you did not misinterpret my response about travel. For the record, I would be willing to do all the necessary traveling for the job." Some interviewers have told us that they have consistently hired those who wrote follow-up notes.

Job Hint 10

"What I do after the interview is give the person my card and tell him or her to call me. It's a test to see if they are committed, how long it takes for them to call, and whether they even call at all."

Another strategy, if you are especially interested in a position, is to ask your references to call on your behalf. Within two hours of her departure, one woman asked two references to call her interviewer. The interviewer was so impressed with the applicant's obvious interest in the job and the caliber of her references, that after speaking with the references she called her right back and hired her.

A Final Word—Outcomes

What if you are offered the job on the spot, during the interview? Do you know what to do in that case?

The following questions will help you analyze whether or not you want to accept a particular job. Take your time with your response. If you are not sure, ask to have some time to think it over. Many applicants take a few hours or even days to decide.

1. Does the job seem suited to me?
2. Was I impressed with the company and the operation?
3. Is the atmosphere one in which I can feel comfortable?
4. Did the other employees seem to like their work?
5. Is the company a growing and financially sound one?
6. Does the company offer training and/or good promotional opportunities?
7. Is the salary and benefit package what I should expect?
8. Do I have enough information to make an informed decision?

On the other hand, what if you are turned down? No one likes to be rejected, even if they really did not want the job. Keeping in mind, however, that the interview is a learning experience, learn from those inevitable *I'm sorry but*s . . . Inquire exactly why you were turned down. Hearing negative things about yourself is no fun, but you should ask—it's to your benefit. You are not trying to change the interviewer's mind and so, again, do not be defensive. As one recruiter put it, "What do you have to lose? If I say to you, 'Well, you didn't have enough experience,' you can respond with 'In what area?' Find out what you need to know to do a better interview next time. So what if I don't like you?" Learn all you can from the interview experience. If you are being sent out by an employment agency, ask them to find out why you weren't hired. Or take a deep breath and make the call yourself, saying, "I realize that you decided to hire someone else, but I would appreciate it if you could give me

some suggestions on how I could improve future interviews."
After all, no interview is a complete failure; some just don't lead
to jobs.

Note:

No interview is over until you have sent a thank-you note.
No interview is over until you have sent a thank-you note.
No interview is over until you have sent a thank-you note.
No interview is over until you have sent a thank-you note.
                                        —*The Three Boxes of Life,* by
                                        Richard Bolles, p. 292

Use a form like this to keep a record of each interview. You
can adapt this one for your notebook or copy it.

Interview Record Form

Before the Interview:

Company _____

Address _____

_____(Room)_____

Travel Instructions _____

_____

_____

Time _____Date _____

Phone No. _____

Person to see _____

Referred to company by _____

After the Interview:

Interviewed by _____

Title _____

Type of company _____

Title of position _____

Salary discussed _____

Positive/negative feelings _____

_____

_____

Notes:

Follow-Up:

What is the next step? _____

_____

_____

Additional information in thank-you note _____

_____

_____

_____

Sent letter, date _____

Contacted with decision _____

Interview Rating Form

Some leading questions to ask yourself. (Give yourself 10 points for every *yes* answer. No cheating!)

1. Were you on time?
2. Did you establish rapport with your interviewer(s)?
3. Were you able to contain or otherwise deal with your nervousness?
4. Were you dressed appropriately?
5. Within the interview context, did you positively relate your strengths and your accomplishments?
6. Did you display interest in the job?
7. Did you ask the kind of questions that prove you understand the employer's needs?
8. Did you answer most of the questions without any trouble?
9. Did you get all the information you needed before you left?
10. Do you know the next step?

Write a few paragraphs summarizing your performance. What do you think was the interviewer's impression of you? What are you most proud of? How did your research help? What else could you have done better to prepare yourself *before* the interview? Generally, how could you have improved this interview (specify some of the ways)? _____

_____

_____

_____

_____

_____

_____

By the Way . . .

Margaret did not get the job at the chemical company. When she called, Ms. Green told her that although they really liked her, they had hired someone with more accounting experience. Margaret didn't get the third job she applied for either. But she did land a job on her fourth interview. The entire process took two months and about $150, including two parking tickets, baby-sitters (and day care), a briefcase, and a new dress. According to Margaret, it was well worth it. She now has a job as a bookkeeper in the bursar's office at the local university. The salary is a little less than she wanted, but the fringe benefits are excellent, since she can now complete her bachelor's degree in accounting—tuition free! She is also delighted with the "spirited" atmosphere of academia. This new job marks a deservedly good new beginning for our friend Margaret Peters.

Congratulations to Margaret, and to you. Today just might be your day to land the job you want!

CATALYST, centered in New York City, has developed over the past 18 years a National Network of Resource Centers which offer educational and career counseling, job referral and placement services for women at over 150 local branches. Catalyst provides career information and self-guidance material to women, interprets the needs of the marketplace to advisors of undergraduate women across the country, helps the employed woman respond effectively to opportunities for upward mobility, assists employers with recruitment, assimilations and advancement for women, and makes research findings and an informed perspective available to legislators, educators, personnel offices and the media.

MONEY TALKS!
How to get it and How to keep it!

☐ 05181 STALKING THE HEADHUNTER, John Tarrant $17.95
a Bantam hardcover

Years ago, the word "headhunter" was almost derogatory. Now it is a respectable euphemism for an executive recruiter and these professionals are becoming more and more the standard agent in the search to fill key, high-level positions in today's corporate world. Seeking out these recruiters and knowing how to deal with them effectively is the idea behind this informative guide to career advancement.

STALKING THE HEADHUNTER deals with specific questions such as when you should play hard-to-get and how to make the recruiter your ally. It also provides a list of over 100 of the most active recruiters and offers discussions on what headhunters look for, how to achieve visibility outside of your company and other fundamental topics.

☐ 34322 THE WORLD-CLASS EXECUTIVE, Chesanow $9.95
a Bantam trade paperback

For the American businessperson in another culture, mistakes or misinterpreted behavior can mean the loss of big contracts. In THE WORLD-CLASS EXECUTIVE, Neil Chesanow offers the first comprehensive guide to negotiating successfully in foreign countries.

Beginning with an overview of the cultures of Western Europe, the Arab world, East Asia, and Latin America, this insightful work reveals the intricate, sometimes subtle rules of behavior in these cultures which are often overlooked or misunderstood by the American executive. It also focuses on the particular problems women executives face, plus tactics female negotiators can adopt to win the cooperation of foreign peers who may be unused to dealing with a woman. No executive, male or female, who must represent his or her company abroad can afford to be without this book.

Look for them at your bookstore us use this coupon for ordering:

Color Wonderful

JoAnne Nicholson and Judy Lewis-Crum

A revolutionary new system of finding your best colors, by the founders of Color 1 Associates.

- How to create an individual color profile and coordinate wardrobe colors with those of your skin, hair, eyes and lips.

- How to choose makeup, jewelry and accessories that compliment your coloring.

- How to salvage the "wrong" color choices in your closet by using the right color accents.

- How color can be used as a tool in your quest for career or personal success . . .

And much, much more in this lavishly illustrated trade format paperback.

COLOR WONDERFUL

Available wherever Bantam Books are sold or use this handy coupon for ordering:

Special Offer
Buy a Bantam Book
for only 50¢.

Now you can have Bantam's catalog filled with hundreds of titles plus take advantage of our unique and exciting bonus book offer. A special offer which gives you the opportunity to purchase a Bantam book for only 50¢. Here's how!

By ordering any five books at the regular price per order, you can also choose any other single book listed (up to a $5.95 value) for just 50¢. Some restrictions do apply, but for further details why not send for Bantam's catalog of titles today!

Just send us your name and address and we will send you a catalog!